AN UNUSUAL LEGACY

Random
Wit and
Recall from
a Life Well
Lived

HOWARD G. PERETZ

ISBN: 978-1-955622-12-7 (hardcover)
978-1-955622-11-0 (paperback)

Edited by Jon Goldberg

Mary Engelbreit artwork on pages 181 and 384 used with written permission from Mary Engelbreit Studios.

Published by
Fideli Publishing, Inc.
119 W. Morgan St.
Martinsville, IN 46151

www.FideliPublishing.com

DEDICATION

"I want to be thoroughly used up when I die, for the harder I work, the more I live."

— George Bernard Shaw

George Bernard Shaw, an Irish playwright and political activist, lived from 1856-1950 and wrote sixty plays, among them *Man and Superman, Pygmalion* (which *My Fair Lady* is based upon), and *Saint Joan.* He won the Nobel Prize for Literature in 1925, and lived in a manner that I totally admire. He once said, "I rejoice in life for its own sake. Life is no brief candle to me. It is part of a splendid torch which I have ahold of for the moment, and I want to make it burn as brightly before handing it over to the next generation."

My own interpretation of Shaw's quote: don't ever contemplate retiring; keep pushing the envelope, and endeavor to become more productive when accomplishing your goals because it becomes more and more challenging the older you get.

ACKNOWLEDGMENTS

Normally, the author would start his acknowledgment page with a thank you to all participants directly involved in book creation and printing. I have decided to put the larger picture individuals I have encountered during the journey at the end of the page.

This book is a tribute to people in general: the important and unimportant, the good and bad. Many people from my life appear in the book, while others remain in my memory, but regardless, all contributed to the person I am today.

One of my pet-peeves, which goes against everything we were taught in school and church and believe in, is that all people are created equal. Nothing could be further from the truth. Significantly, all people are unique and different. If we were all alike, there would not be anything to write about. I can't imagine a world where sameness trumps individuality; how boring life would be if you went outside and all you saw were Howard Peretz duplicates.

Now to the acknowledgment of those individuals directly involved in creating this work, in alphabetical order by first name.

Ally Lacours, a young lady at Life Is Good clothing brand, who pushed to get a custom shirt done for my photo on the back cover of the book, once she learned how important their shirts were to my cancer recovery.

Darrie Ichilov, physical therapist extraordinaire, who runs Advanced Medical Therapy and who, after learning about many of my life experiences, urged me to write this book.

Dawn Madsen, perhaps the biggest fan of my books, who I visit with every Saturday night at the neighborhood eatery Pinnacle Grille, where she both waits and manages.

Derek Gable, who lives the life in Rancho Palos Verde but still makes time to tutor young people, invent toys, and assist me as I go from project to project.

Hendrik Hannemann, my computer geek who demonstrates patience as I call him regularly with questions—some serious some dumb—and he always solves the problem.

Jon Goldberg, my youthful book editor with a stated love of grammar (my nemesis), trained in *the Chicago Manual of Style.*

Milan Mermall, my best friend who gets me away from the book grind by having lunch with me once a week for 12 years, where it has been traditional to close each meal with a hand of liars poker.

Paula Bower, a retired photographer and fellow yoga student who as a friend took this old fart before the camera for a cover shot, making him look respectable.

Robin Surface, publisher in Indiana who knows the self-publishing business inside out and, importantly, the inner workings of Amazon, the gorilla in the room.

"Ry" Cooder, best known for playing the slide guitar, who covered Lead Belly's *Goonight Irene* with his band in 1977; it was the best recording of the tune that I listen to at the conclusion of each writing day.

Steve Rothschild, life blood of the sports group at Sun City, who has allowed and encouraged me to do book signings, especially those one-liners that have become one of my staples.

Geri, the Yoga Princess

INTRODUCTION

When I was young, everyone would ponder who won the game of life: the individual with the most toys at the end, or the individual who left with an empty toy chest. Focusing solely on materialism was very much in fashion, but as I aged—I recently turned eighty-three—the question of legacy and what I have accomplished while on this planet has become the larger and more appropriate question for consideration.

My wonderful late brother-in-law, Steve Draizin, who passed much too early, thought much about the subject and left a significant legacy: his wife Dolly, two children, and five grandchildren. Steve was rich monetarily but also spiritually—he read his bar mitzvah haftorah at age thirteen, and at age seventy, he recited the identical haftorah.

On the surface, my legacy (measured by traditional thinking) is a bit disappointing and a mixed bag. At the top of the spectrum of life, I checked the boxes: I was married to the same woman, Geri—my Yoga Princess—for sixty-one years; we are one-percenters; we have a son and daughter, Lauren (happily married to Dave), and Michael (happily married to Karen), both of whom are loving and smart and financially independent; we have four college-age grandchildren: Henry, James, Will, and Katey, who all have their heads screwed on straight. On the downside, I did not properly prepare financially for retirement, and have become partially dependent on my offspring.

My legacy is still intact, but I still need to wake up each day with a purpose; and given my current skill set, it would be to write another book. To date, I have penned five books— mostly about sports. On my last birthday (August 30), I began thinking about my legacy as a subject matter for my next publication, wondering if I have something to contribute beyond family and friends while at the same time not stroking my ego. I have gone out of my way to be open and honest throughout the text: "start taking off the armor."

At my fiftieth wedding anniversary celebration, I wrote an essay about the most treasured moments of marriage to Geri and discovered a common thread—all were humorous. Conclusion: focus on humor and you can reach into the memory vault still intact.

The work *UNUSUAL LEGACY: Random Wit and Recall From a Life Well Lived* is divided into four parts: Kith and Kin; Elbow Grease; Fun and Frolic; and Witty Repartee. There are 156 short, entertaining, diverse vignettes dating from the 1940s to the present, with photos where pertinent and available. LOL

Howard G. Peretz
The Old School Sports Junkie
peretzhoward@gmail.com
Cave Creek, Arizona
April 2023

TABLE OF CONTENTS

PART ONE
KITH AND KIN

PART TWO
ELBOW GREASE

PART THREE
FUN AND FROLIC

PART FOUR
WITTY REPARTEE

PART ONE

KITH AND KIN

*"I haven't got a Cadillac.
I've got a subway token."*
—Nipsey Russell

NYC SUBWAY ODDITIES

G rowing up in the Da Bronx—one of the five boroughs—my gateway to Manhattan was the *Pelham IRT* line. I often took the subway for granted, not thinking about the 665 track miles along the mainline or which stations in the Bronx were elevated.

Everything inside the subway appeared normal: you could transfer at no cost to any one of the thirty-six lines, and trains ran frequently, though you would often stand during rush hour. There was a manned coin booth (platform tokens didn't start until 1953), and graffiti was absent (it didn't arrive until 1969). Maps were displayed in each car, and apart from an occasional turn-style jumper, there was no crime. I never saw a subway cop hanging out on the platform. And youngsters would roam the cars, providing entertainment before passing the hat around for contributions.

But as you would anticipate, there were a handful of out-of-the-ordinary experiences that have remained with me after all these years.

On a New York subway
you get fined for spitting,
but you can throw up for nothing.
— Lewis Grizzard

"DO YOU HAVE
A YOUNG BLONDE-HAIRED BOY?"

Dad and I were on our way home, entering the subway at the 42nd Street Grand Central Station. There were some seats open, but no two next to each other, so we sat across from each other. Many stations later, I looked up to see Dad, and noticed every passenger looked the same; all adult males, attired with navy overcoats and gray dress hats and the *NY Times* opened for reading.

I was understandably too timid and shy at age seven to poke each stranger on the shoulder, so instead I asked the man sitting closest if a man that I described had left the train.

He responded that he just got off. So off I ran, just making it before the doors closed.

When I got to the platform, I realized the stranger had been mistaken; and I was alone on the platform (later learning it was the Brook Avenue and 138th Street Station). It was among the most deserted stations on the line. I was smart enough to go to the change booth, and an engaged, welcoming, middle-aged cashier—understanding my circumstances—asked for my phone number, which luckily I remembered and promptly gave him.

He called my home. Mother answered. When she heard the words: "Do you have a young, blonde-haired boy?" she just about fainted (or so she told me later). The cashier agreed to keep me in the booth until the Lone Ranger arrived. Subsequently, Dad, after many stations, realized he had lost his only child and called home. Learning of my location, he arrived shortly thereafter, hugged me, and thanked the cashier. Off to Westchester Avenue Station we went on the next local train heading North.

When we arrived home, I watched as Mom gave Dad holy hell for the first time. It would be a long time before Dad was allowed out with me on a similar journey without Mom coming too.

SUBWAY DOORS UNPREDICTABLE

It didn't matter that when one train left, another soon arrived: passengers still raced to get on the train before it departed. Passengers who just got on board would hold the doors open until the last possible second. That was part of the game. The look on the faces of those who made it was pure joy.

A group of buddies and I were returning from a short camping trip (believe it or not) by subway. We smelled and carried dirty duffel bags, but the train was empty. We stood near the doors, just hanging out. Of the four of us, David Landau was the most mischievous of the group: a wise guy who often got in the face of anyone who engaged him, regardless of the person's size.

This time, we watched one of NY's finest sights: a policeman racing to make the train. The doors were about to close as the cop charged, and Dave held the doors open. The cop was just a few feet from entering, but at the last minute, David let the doors close, giving the cop the middle finger.

What happened next was indescribable: the doors opened, the cop reached into the car, and grabbing David by the neck, dragged him onto the platform. The train took off without David or the cop, and we all laughed more than we had in our three days of camping. After all, we were city guys, and camping was hard work without the conveniences of home.

David and I are still friends all these years later. It's hard to imagine that Dave became a successful psychiatrist, residing in Albuquerque, New Mexico, advising patients on how to behave properly in society, even prescribing medications where needed.

Joe Towbin, left, starred as a swordsman while attending Syracuse University.

LICORICE STICK GOES BYE-BYE

Our parents required we play a musical instrument. Accordion was selected for me because it had keys much like a piano and we had no room for a piano in our apartment. Twice a week, I took the bus to the Vinnie Roberts Studio on Castle Hill Avenue, dreading every moment but continuing to go because I was respectful of my parents' wishes.

A big break came when we reached the moment of truth: renting the instrument was not at all practical, and Mother said if I wanted to continue, she would be pleased to purchase the instrument. After a few seconds, I said no thanks, and I was free to work on my stick-ball hitting broomsticks, courtesy of Leroy the porter.

My close friend, Joe Towbin, was not as lucky. His instrument of choice was the clarinet—affectionately known as the licorice stick single-reed woodwind instrument—and he was good enough to play in the James Monroe orchestra, led by the flamboyant Dr. Firestone.

Then the fateful day came: Joe, upon exiting the train at the Parkchester elevated train station, was unable to dislodge his clarinet from between the train doors. The train went on its way with Joe in hot pursuit; but alas, Joe could not outrun the train, and when he got to the end of the platform, the clarinet disappeared, never to be seen again.

Instead of becoming a musician, Joe became a successful dentist, recently retired after practicing in Greenwich Village, NYC, for over fifty years.

"SONNY-BOY, YOU LOOK BETTER WITHOUT THE HAT"

In 1960, after turning twenty-one, I was selected by Martha Scudder to join the Bloomingdale's Summer Executive Training Program. I thought I was on my way to becoming a tycoon, even though I was getting paid the same salary as a clerk.

To celebrate the occasion, I purchased a few trinkets at the store and then went clothes shopping. I wanted to arrive at my first day of work looking good. So I bought a Brooks Bros. three-piece suit, a button-down dress shirt with a repp tie (diagonally-striped silk tie), Johnson and Murphy wingtips, and a Stetson Fedora hat.

I decided to don this new attire before heading home on the train. Bloomingdales was located at 59th Street and Lexington, and the trip home was approximately forty-five minutes.

The train (as anticipated) was packed—not a single seat was open. As it moved further North, the train began to empty, and whenever seats opened up, a chivalrous executive tipped his hat, pointing some ladies to the open seats. By the time we got to the Bronx, the train was largely empty, but I was still basking in my standing glory.

Then three pre-teen boys sitting together indicated they were getting off at the next stop and invited me to sit down. I took them up on their offer, and off went the train. Then the most amazing theft happened; my seat was in front of an open window, and one of the boys reached over, taking the hat off my head! Could it be? I was no longer an executive!

I felt stupid, and a nice, middle-aged woman sitting across the aisle made matters even worse: "Don't feel bad, sonny, you look better without the hat!"

I'M NOT YELLING I'M JEWISH

SECTION 2

OY VEY!

I am most proud of my Jewish heritage, dating to childhood, where three generations resided in a five-room apartment. It was a rare foyer that included the envy of neighbors, a view of the picturesque oval, but just one bathroom to share among the five of us. And air conditioning was light years away.

My first sense of being Jewish was that we kept a kosher household, which meant my favorite foods, bacon (from a pig) and shellfish (shrimp), were off limits. I must admit that as I reached double digits, I learned how to cheat outside of the home, where my Yiddish Grandma ruled with an iron fist.

I must confess that while growing up, I knew little about the origins of my faith, apart from knowing that we were a persecuted people who needed to stick together. Interestingly,

I was born on August 30, 1939, the day Hitler marched into Poland, starting World War II.

The big event in a Jewish boy's life is the bar mitzvah celebration, where upon reading the Torah at age thirteen he becomes a man. Reading from the Torah written in Hebrew was a terrifying experience as the Temple elders would stand in the back and shake their heads if you made a single mistake.

To prepare, I was required to attend Sunday school, where the Jewish religion was taught. But, all us kids cared about was the big day. The week before my big day, my friend Stephen fainted on the way to the Bimah Lectern (a fancy podium to where we would read from the Torah). He never did manage to make it through, but I did. This meant I got gelt or money from all who attended, as well as first crack at pigs-in-the-blanket. And, most importantly, no more Sunday school!

Upon reflection, at age thirteen I hardly felt like a man. What's worse, my lifestyle and rules at home didn't change one bit.

CAFETERIA JEW QUITE OKAY

A cafeteria Jew is someone who, like me, picks and chooses from the religious menu: high holidays payments; "as you go" Temple attendance, rather than being a permanent member of the congregation; marrying a Shana Madala (a Yiddish Jewish expression meaning a pretty girl); a Sunday breakfast consisting of a smear of cream cheese on a fresh, warm, hand-twisted, onion bagel (not an air-blown, fraudulent Einstein bagel), topped with high-priced belly or nova lox.

There's also Sunday night Chinese food; ala the Buddy Hackett menu (so much from column A and so much from column B); traditional foods for Passover, like macaroons, matzoh, and matzoh-ball soup, with balls as hard as a baseball, and gefilte fish with horseradish; hosting a lavish Bar or Bat Mitzvah if you have children, and then the weddings later; living in areas where there is a satisfactory percentage of Jews; Jewish Summer Camp either in the Catskills, Lakewood or the Poconos; mandatory college graduation from a top tier university; voting for Jewish candidates for public office; and later in life, moving to Florida, and living lavishly in a condo in Boca until the very end.

Part of my rationale for becoming a Cafeteria Jew was because, above all else, we were encouraged to assimilate into the American culture. We wanted to be Americans, not "hyphenated" Jewish-Americans.

In thinking about assimilation, I remember being struck by the news that Nabisco's Oreo cookies would become kosher in 1997, earning the "OU" seal, as required by the group that represents Orthodox Jewish congregations around the country. Clearly, Jews had arrived; we were now equal. The only question remaining: how to eat the Oreo and separate the top and bottom; did we lick off the icing, or simply bite into the cookie?

JUBU DOES EXIST

A JUBU is defined as a Jewish person who finds fulfill-
ment in Buddhist philosophy and practices but has not
given up their Jewish identity. Research indicates that
up to 30 percent of American Buddhists, mostly from the baby
boomer generation, identify as such. I must admit that I have
never met or known anyone other than myself who considers
themselves a JUBU, although there is a 2007 paperback titled
Jew in the Lotus by Rodger Kamenetz.

Among my favorite Buddhist sayings, which I repeat daily
upon awakening, are the following: nothing to hold onto is
the root of happiness; the path is the goal, the path is unchar-
tered; your power ends where your fear begins; keep the door

open without expectations; pain is not a punishment, pleasure is not a reward; patience is pleasure; don't expect applause; patience implies a willingness to be alive rather than seek harmony; between birth and death we are all alone; turn arrows into flowers; as long as you're wishing for things to change, they never will; start taking off that armor.

MUSICIAN STING TALKS ABOUT GOD, HITS CLOSE TO HOME

My father and best friend, Milton, died unexpectedly when I was just eighteen years old and away at college. It was the most traumatic moment of my life and has affected me ever since. The hurt and pain was so deep that I have buried my feeling about Dad, never crying out loud. Religion at the time offered no solace.

I was a regular viewer of the *Actors Studio* television show, hosted by James Lipton, on Bravo for twenty-two years (1994-2017). Lipton was a superb interviewer, unlike any other, and the show's long format was unique (guests were on-air for a full hour). The show was praised in a *New York Times* article: "In Mr. Lipton's guest chair, actors cease being stars, instead becoming artists and teachers."

Among his guests was the musician Sting, a solo singer and member of the band The Police. Sting, a fantastic songwriter, played guitar and was a winner of seventeen Grammy awards. In addition, he was a noted humanitarian.

On Lipton's show, Sting provided such an incredible moment. Lipton was fond of word association, and when he asked Sting about God, Sting replied: "God killed my mother" (she had died of cancer in 1986). Sting's simple answer hit home. I am, however, convinced there is a Creator, but he or she is hard to identify; there is also a natural order of things, and the existence of God, while a much heavier burden to contemplate, is certainly within the realm of possibility.

BUILDING FUND:
BIGGEST PROBLEM JEWS FACE

When I turned forty-eight, the same year my father passed, I was having a bad year career-wise and leaning towards depression; I learned this was not an uncommon occurrence. I realized that I needed a spiritual awakening and decided to give Judaism another chance—after an absence of thirty years.

I spoke by phone to the Rabbi of Temple Emanu-El in Westfield, New Jersey, where we had resided. It was an upscale, conservative congregation of 1,100 families. The Rabbi was most enthusiastic and offered to visit Dad's burial plot in Westwood, New Jersey—a plot that I had never visited and sadly hadn't paid to maintain.

We first met at the rabbi's temple office. He was not what I expected. I suppose I was looking for someone who reminded me of my first rabbi, Rabbi Lublin, who was old, had a long white beard, and was all about touching and hugging. The Rabbi at the temple in Westfield, on the other hand, was perfectly dressed in business attire, from his three-piece suit to his Nicole Miller tie, button-down shirt, and winged-tipped shoes.

He was the perfect host and gentleman and asked me what questions I had. I started with what I thought was a soft ball, a smart and broad question: What is the biggest problem facing the Jews today? The rabbi said the building fund. He then showed me a wall chart of monies received and monies needed to complete the renovation and expansion—he had a long way to go. I got up, thanked him for his time, and walked out. I was completely dismayed. Organized Judaism was no longer a possibility for me.

COMEDIAN JACKIE MASON
SAME ON STAGE AND OFF

I fell in love with stand-up comedian Jackie Mason after watching his 1986 one-man show, *According to Me* on Broadway. I was not alone, as Jackie won both Tony and Emmy awards and was also nominated for a Grammy. One *Time Magazine* critic had this to say: "Throughout his career, Mason spoke to [his] audience."

With the Yiddish intonations of an immigrant who just completed a course in English, one of his best jokes was this: "It is easy to tell the difference between Jews and Gentiles. After the show, all the gentiles are saying, 'Have a drink? I want a drink. Let's have a drink!' While all the Jew's are saying, 'Have you eaten yet? Want a piece of cake? Let's have some cake.'"

One day, while having dinner at a 57th Street West Side eatery with my wife and friends, I was about to be served my favorite New York Cheesecake—you can tell it's genuine if you put a fork in it and the cake rises, as this one did. I looked outside, and there on the corner by the phone booth was Jackie holding court. I excused myself, forgetting about my manners and dessert, and went to engage Jackie in typical shtick. This was when I realized his genius also extended to body movements and gestures. It was one of the highlights of my life.

Jewish comedians were always front and center in my life, from the time my parents took me to the Borscht Belt (also known as the Catskills). There I saw Henny Youngman, master of the one-liner, and the great storyteller Alan King, with lighted cigar in his hand. In 1978, *Time Magazine* claimed that 80 percent of all stand-up comedians in the United States were Jewish.

There are too many Jewish comedians to list, but I would be doing a disservice if I didn't mention my favorites: Mason, Hackett, Youngman, King, Larry David, Groucho Marx, Jerry Lewis, Howard Stern, Jon Stewart, Mel Brooks, Billy Crystal, Sid Caesar, Jack Benny, Robert Klein, Carl Reiner, Bob Saget, Mort Sahl, Gene Wilder, Jerry Seinfeld, Jack Black, Danny Kaye, Lenny Bruce, Sarah Silverman, Adam Sandler, Joan Rivers, Don Rickles, Bette Midler, Rodney Dangerfield, and Milton Berle.

Today, political correctness has us laughing less, and stand-up comedians have largely disappeared, as most everything funny is offensive to someone or some group. I admit, however, that at the top of the comedy pyramid are two non-Jews: George Carlin and Jonathan Winters. My favorite Carlin routine includes criticizing too much stuff by promoting a new term "minimalism," and complaining about the stupidity of golf and the absurdity of taking acres of prime land to hit a stationery ball into a hole. Winters won me over when he performed an unrehearsed skit and then did an entire routine live on the *Tonight Show*. He was a guest on that show many times over the years.

mishpacha (meesh-pah-CHAH)
  n. (Hebrew) family

    (Yiddish) the entire family network of relatives by
    blood or marriage (and sometimes close friends);
    "she invited the whole mishpocha"

Grandkids at the age they were most precious, top to bottom,
Katey, Will, Henry, James

SECTION 3

MISHPACHA

As an only child, I grew up surrounded by adults: grandmother, father (who went to war when I was four years old), mother, and mother's sister. There was also Barney, my grandfather, who died early on and whom I remember little about apart from that he wore a truss, also known as a hernia support belt, and a handful of piggy backs. When he died at the hospital, I remember my grandmother blaming it on the hospital, certain that she could have done a better job and kept him alive.

My mother's brother, Harry, a largely uneducated but hard-working man, ran a paint store. He came by our house weekly for dinner. My dad's family consisted of two married sisters, one with a daughter Gail, who lived in New Jersey; the other, Bea, married my Uncle Mac, who was a man's man and served in World War II under General Patton. Mac became a unionized assembly worker at the Ford Plant in Mahwah.

Charlotte, Bea's sister, was a hoot, but her husband, Al, left a lot to be desired. He changed his name from Pritzker to Price to hide his Jewishness, then he joined a mason-fraternal group that believed in a Supreme Being—or Grand Architect—of the Universe. Plus, to avoid military service in World War II, he shot himself in the leg.

Once I married Geri, I moved away from Parkchester and had two kids— Lauren Joy and Michael James—three years apart. They were both born in Boston but were raised in LA until we moved to New Jersey, where they finished their high school education. To my dismay, the wife and kids preferred Westfield to Encino, California, because they fell in love with the quaint, picturesque colonial town.

Both Lauren and Michael have blessed me with two grandkids, each of whom are now in college. Henry Eisen, is a political science major at Colgate, and Will Eisen, is a biochemistry major at William and Mary. James Peretz, is studying nuclear engineering at Penn. State, and Katey Peretz, is a liberal arts major at Lafayette.

Grandma Lena my first roommate.

GRANDMA LENA:
TOUGHEST BROAD I EVER KNEW

My first roommate was my grandma Lena. We were an unlikely pair, as I was going to nursery school while she ran the household, made all the meals and did all the housework. She spoke mostly Yiddish, but after a while, I understood her.

My most vivid memories include seeing her take her teeth out at night and place them in a glass filled with some type of antiseptic, and also, in the morning, with assistance from my mother, fitting her way into a girdle.

She was one tough cookie. She alone was allowed into the kitchen, and did all the shopping, refusing assistance. After years of everyone asking her to, grandma finally agreed to have a cleaning woman come in weekly. Grandma was a bit of a racist, referring to this woman as a Shvartze. She followed the her around cleaning up behind her. When she was advised the cleaning woman was entitled to lunch, she gave her two slices of bread and one slice of cheese.

I accompanied Grandma regularly to the kosher butcher on White Plains Road, who she affectionately referred to as "Gaier the Goniff" (Goniff means *crook*) because Gaier was known to put his thumb on the scale with chicken and meat charged by the pound. Grandma caught him in the act once, picked up a butcher knife and followed him into the freezer where she proceeded to get even.

My grandmother prided herself on covering the plate with an abundance of food; never did I see the actual plate. The problem was her food was overcooked, especially when it came to fish. She also didn't see so well, so the first task was to avoid the bones, some visible, others not. When it came to plating, the eyes of the fish were always facing you because the eyes were considered a delicacy. The biggest problem, though, was that the fish was dry; but Grandma said, "Howard, it can't be dry, it comes from the ocean."

Grandma Lena did, however, make me laugh regularly, largely because of her difficulty with the English language. She was a regular reader of *Forward*, a weekly Jewish newspaper. When she read something of interest, she couldn't wait to share; the problem was that the *Forward* article was ancient news—a week late—but we played along, not willing to rain on her parade.

A funny aside: she was a loyal *Perry Mason* viewer. She was in awe of his legal brilliance, never realizing that he never lost a case because he had smart writers.

Another of my favorite memories is watching Grandma sit on the Parkchester benches with her two best friends, talking about their grandchildren, which was a daily topic. While one of the grandchildren studied law and the other was attending Medical school, I was going for my PhD in marketing. No matter how many ways I tried communicating this field of study to grandma, she couldn't comprehend why I needed to go to graduate school to learn how to shop. She'd ask, "Isn't marketing just shopping?"

TANTE ROSE
LOVE PLUS MONEY, BETTER THE
SECOND TIME AROUND

Tante Rose was the oldest of the three Scher girls and the most beautiful. She had an opportunity to star as a glamorous Zigfeld Girl, but grandma wouldn't allow a showgirl in the family. Tante resided on Riverside Drive, and to my surprise, her apartment had a balcony that looked out on the Hudson River. My first recollection of the balcony was standing there watching the American soldiers returning from World War II; I was just five years old.

I was also fascinated by her vintage Victrola record player. I spent hours watching the records go 'round and 'round, and to this day, I get choked-up listening to the long version of Walter Houston singing the haunting "September Song."

Soon, Rose moved in with us, and I would discover years later that it was because her husband, Lou, had committed suicide. I also learned before Lou, Rose had fallen in love with Jack Stern, a hunk of a guy who was light in the wallet. Rose told Jack to come back when he had money, and twenty years later, after Lou had passed away, Jack showed up with a large checkbook, and they lived happily ever after.

Later, when I was living in LA, I went to Miami Beach on a business trip. While I was there, I hoped to see Rose, who was now living alone at Morton Towers Apartments. I hadn't seen in a long time. I called her, told her I was in town, and asked if I could buy her dinner. She said, "No, it's poker night and I can't go." The group she played with was dying off, and were down to only four players—without her, there would be no game.

Tante Rose had always had a deep affection for gambling, often betting on the Irish Sweepstakes and going to the dog track, where she bet on the greyhound who had pooped last before the race.

MOM SYLVIA:
PRAGMATIC DECISION MAKER

My mother, Sylvia, always had her feet on the ground. She survived the unexpected death of her first husband at age forty-eight. At ninety-five, when life no longer felt fun, she instructed me "no tubes." She then went to the beauty parlor for the last time and sent a clear signal that it was time to go: she said no to a dish of chocolate ice cream, one of her favorites (though coffee was her absolute favorite flavor).

After losing her first husband, Mom explained that she was just looking for companionship—not even a loving relationship. She wanted my support in finding someone, which I gladly gave. So, when she had dates, I did a drive-by. I'd drop

Mom off, drive around the block, and wait for the signal telling me whether or not to stay. She ended up ice skating at Rockefeller Center, dancing at Roseland, and so on. She also went on many cruises with her friend Mina Gordon.

Finally, she reached her desired goal: she married Sam Schilling, who wanted to retire to Arizona and take her with him. (He always referred to Arizona as God's Country, and that's where I currently live). However, Mother held out for Miami Beach. Florida was her calling. After Sam passed, her third husband, Alfred, turned out to be a jewel. I was pleased to call him Dad.

One day, I was to meet Alfred at the NYC Essex House, so I flew in from LA for the occasion, but we had difficulty connecting. I knew they both were staying there, but Mother had neglected to provide her new married name, so I had to wait in the lobby for hours until the elevator door opened and there she was. She and Alfred were happily married for over thirty-five years.

One of the best examples of Mother's pragmatism was my wedding. The wedding was in my apartment (9C) and it was conducted in three parts: her friends were invited at noon; mid-afternoon was for family; and evening was time for my friends. Cleverly, there was one caterer, one hall.

With envelopes full of cash, because there were no wedding registers or gift cards at the time, my wife and I honeymooned in Europe for six weeks with the proceeds. We realized deep down that we would never again get six weeks for a vacation.

As we left on our cruise ship, we were interviewed by Gabe Pressman of NBC-TV New York (the premier local NYC broadcaster on NBC for over sixty years). Gabe asked how we liked our accommodations, and my wife answered, "Not very much because we have bunk beds!" From the dock, we yelled to our family, but to no avail—the interview was never seen by anyone we knew.

The only dumb thing I ever saw Mom do, apart from not being able to parallel park, was when I received an emergency call from the Pelham Bay public golf course, where she had been playing. She said the car wouldn't start. I arrived, inspected the car, and advised her that someone had stolen her tires; no wonder the car wouldn't start.

I INHERITED DAD MILTON'S GIFT OF GAB

Everyone told me that I was just like Dad, both in appearance and temperament. I took this as the ultimate compliment. In addition to being my dad, he was also my best friend.

I always loved it when he asked me to keep a secret from Mom. For example, he promised not to smoke cigars in the living room, and when the ashes fell, he rubbed them into

Dad Milton

the carpet and moved his favorite chair forward to cover the spot. The problem with this strategy was that over time, the space between the TV and chair disappeared, and he got caught.

My most treasured memory of him was when we arrived in Burlington, Vermont, for my second year of college at UVM. He told me to take the night off, suggesting I spend it with my brothers at the fraternity house, and then he and Mom would see me in the morning for breakfast.

At the house, we kept a list of "townies." A townie was a high school co-ed who was easily impressed by a college student, especially if the student was from a big city like New York. If I called one of these young ladies at the last moment; it would be a night of petting and perhaps getting to second base.

This night, we were to meet downtown near the Park Café. When she got there, she was one of the most unattractive teenagers I had ever seen. She was tall and thin with no bust to speak of and she was wearing a large cross around her neck that glowed in the dark. I decided I couldn't be seen with her, so the solution was to hide her at the local movie house, which was playing *A Thousand Clowns* starring Jason Robards.

It was midweek, and the theater was largely empty, except for a couple behind me. The couple turned out to be my parents. Dad gave me a thumbs-up, but Mom hid her eyes, finding the encounter not funny in the least.

Geri demonstrates how to drink beer in Munich.

FIRST WIFE PASSES FOR SECOND WIFE: IS THAT A GOOD THING FOR THE HUSBAND?

I must admit that when I was twenty-two years old, I was all about outer beauty (even though inner beauty is, of course, where it's at). Geri was a Parkchester and neighborhood girl, and dating a neighborhood girl was considered an act of desperation.

I had never dated a neighborhood girl before. But Geri was a looker and a modern dancer, the token white in the avant-garde Alvin Ailey Dance Company. She had been dating a friend of mine, Donald Schiff, but they stopped dating, and as a custom, I asked his permission to date her. He said, "You can have her."

Our first date was on a school night. She did floor exercises for the entire evening—mostly splits—while I watched, making polite conversation.

I asked about going on a second date the following Saturday night. Geri said, "That's the most special night of the week, and you have to 'work my way up the list' before you can claim that night." I am super competitive, and never realized the trap that had been laid. A few months later, we married.

Though we've been happily married for sixty-one years, neither Geri nor I remember me proposing. There was, however, a significant event: my good friend, Arnold Green, was getting married—a Christmas wedding—and I could take Geri as my plus one if we were serious. I guess our going to the wedding together became the de facto proposal.

Years later, our daughter's friends would say, "Your Mom is hot." Geri repeatedly lied about her age, and as a result, over time she became younger than her daughter.

When I went through a midlife crisis, and at the suggestion of a co-worker, I started taking yoga classes. My instructor was Nicole Mode, based in Garwood, New Jersey. Nicole was French through and through, with an accompanying accent—

and very spiritual, too. She made a believer out of me; I was in a much better place.

Nicole sponsored summer weekend yoga trips at the Frost Valley YMCA in Liberty, New York. It was the perfect retreat: morning, afternoon, and evening yoga classes, hiking in the woods, late night snacks, folk music, and, most importantly, a wooden cabin next to a brook with gourmet food and no television or phones.

I invited Geri to this weekend, and she immediately became Nicole's star pupil. Following the trip, Geri became a certified yoga instructor, and she taught restorative and beginner yoga for over thirty-five years. She is a superb instructor and is still teaching. I call her the *Yoga Princess* because she is beautiful both inside and out, and always looking the part.

THE ART OF LIVING

"You think I'm teaching ballet
but really I'm teaching the art of living."
—Shelia Rozann, daughter Lauren's ballet teacher

We pushed our daughter into ballet. Geri had been a dancer, and Lauren followed suit. She was driven even at a young age, and her goal was to become a principal dancer with the New York City Ballet. Her dancing career began in Chatsworth, a suburb of Los Angeles, at the Rozann Zimmerman school, where she became a top pupil. She never missed daily classes and entered all the local competitions. Judges decided winners and losers because as a dancer, you either have it or you don't—and Lauren had it.

I remember putting her on a plane to San Francisco—she was maybe ten years old—to go off to become a summer apprentice with the San Francisco Ballet. On her first call, upon arrival, she told us it was cold in the city and to send warmer clothes. Her second call was to inform us she had seen her first flasher.

Later on, she danced with the New York City Ballet—also as a summer apprentice—I flew to the city to be interviewed by a patron, who would provide us with no-charge apartment housing.

When Lauren turned fifteen, we moved to New Jersey, and she continued her ballet training. One highlight was when she was selected to play Clara in the *Nutcracker* at the famous Paper Mill Playhouse in Millburn. We went many times to see Lauren perform, and my parents flew in from North Miami Beach, always paying retail. Shortly thereafter, Lauren stopped dancing, and her torso changed completely as a result of eating for the first time in her life.

A pursuit of excellence was the primary lesson of Lauren's ballet experience. She pushed herself academically, and in high school never received a grade below an A. Another valuable by-product from dance was learning how to organize her time. Lauren applied for early admission to Columbia, went co-ed, and got accepted. Her younger brother asked, "Why don't you stop studying?"

Lauren replied, "I'm in school to learn; there will always be time to play."

Lauren probably could have gotten into Harvard. She would often put me in my place, saying that I just wanted to brag to friends and family about her success, whereas she was the one going to college and doing the work.

Today, Lauren is the busiest person I know, excelling at everything she does. She has mastered "the art of living," proving that her first ballet instructor, Sheila Rozann, had it right.

Michael at Shackamaxon Country Club.

IF THERE IS A GOD,
HE'S PROBABLY A SCRATCH GOLFER

My son, Michael, grew up in Encino, California, in the 1970s. He often wore Dodger Blue on his sleeve, and we went regularly to Chavez Ravine, where the Dodgers played. Their infield players stayed on the team throughout the decade: Steve Garvey (his hero), Davy Lopes, Bill Russell, and Ron Cey.

When he was young, would play wiffle ball in front of the house when I got home from work. We followed one simple rule: when Dad says play is over, play is over.

I decided to give Mike baseball lessons at Balboa Park and was fortunate to have come in contact with Tom Gamboa, who at the time was a scout for the Chicago Cubs. Tom was a great instructor, and by the time Michael got to Little League, his fundamentals were off the chart.

(Side note: While Gamboa was coaching first base at the Chicago White Sox's Comiskey Park in 2002, the unthinkable happened: he was viciously attacked by a father and his son, and suffered permanent hearing loss.)

We belonged to the Calabasas Park Tennis Club, so naturally the second sport I pushed Mike toward was tennis. Mike graduated from art classes in the tot lot to taking beginner tennis classes from professional Greg Heinbeck (who my daughter Lauren happened to have a crush on).

We moved to Westfield, New Jersey, in 1981, and Michael excelled on the Junior Varsity baseball team there, and he was awarded MVP.

The town was heavily into high school sports, but it was also dominated by the old boys network. The Varsity Coach decided not to start Michael as a middle infielder, though he was clearly the most talented on the team in that position.

It was the first night of Passover, and we had plans to have Seder in Stamford, Connecticut, where Geri's sister Dollie, Dollie's husband Steve, and their two children, Richard and Jen, lived. At school that day, Michael got word from Varsity Coach Bob Brewster that he would be starting at second base. Understandably, Michael made his case with us to play instead of going to Seder. When mutual friend Rudy Kassinger said he would handle getting Michael to the game, off we went.

During fielding practice, outfielder Clint Factor threw the ball to the infield, and at the precise moment, Michael turned his head and the ball broke his nose. This ended—for all practical purposes—his promising baseball career. Though we were Jewish, we didn't attend Temple, and the issue of "God sending a message" to Michael did not resonate.

Michael still turned out to be a gifted athlete. One of the fondest memories of my sporting career was having Michael join the thirty-five-and-over basketball league with me. We were the first father-son pair to accomplish this feat. I could shoot better, but Michael was nonetheless skilled at every phase of the game. He rarely passed me the ball, though, telling me he didn't have eyes in the back of his head.

Michael's best sport turned out to be golf. He taught himself and became a scratch golfer, blaming me for not giving him golf lessons. He has now become a top executive at A&E Network, combining his golf skills and social skills to master client-focused golf.

While his sister, Lauren, was the better student, Michael's philosophy of being a solid B student while still having a life proved an effective combination. One important note: Michael received an executive diploma from Harvard, so now I can brag and say my son has a degree from Harvard that complements his MBA from Columbia.

Mom: "The only important thing is your health."

DOCTORS ONCE MADE HOUSE CALLS

As my mother smartly said, health is everything, but I rarely heard her because I was too busy chasing green. Now that I'm eighty-three years young and a cancer survivor, I have learned these basic truths: first, as famed news anchor Walter Cronkite remarked, "Getting old is not for sissies;" second, your health is your responsibility, not the doctor's.

As to quality of life and longevity rate, these variables have an order of importance: luck, lifestyle, genetics, and medical care. If you want to live to 106 years old, as the story goes, live to 105 and then proceed cautiously. Here's a good joke to describe the process of aging using few words: When you're young, you want a BMW. When you're old, you want a BM.

The biggest bone I have to pick with the medical community is the neglect of nurturing during treatment. I believe that part is every bit as important as advancements in diagnostic technology. The unintended consequence of privacy rights is the absence of interaction between fellow patients, something that should be at the heart of one's support group. Also, there are so many specialists to see that the primary care doctor—the main man who once made house calls—is now content to act as a "traffic cop," reviewing blood work, writing prescriptions, and recommending specialists, rarely ever touching the patient.

Integrated medicine does not exist. The Western-trained doctor, is about numbers and works as a detail person for the pharmaceutical industry, while the alternative doc is all about prevention through vegan dieting and selling supplements out of the back room, while also opposing powerful drugs like chemotherapy, which "poisons the body to get rid of more severe poisons." If you want integrated care, the patient does the integrating.

When I became cancer free—the best two words in the English language—I attributed my cure to receiving chemotherapy from the west, provided by oncologist Michael Roberts, along with following eastern lifestyle changes from Dr. Ron Peters of Body, Mind, Medicine.

My very bright daughter, in trying to comfort me, says, "As you get older, you take more tests." The problem with this logic is that failing a test in school is one thing, but failing a medical test could be life changing.

HOW EAGLES "DESPERADO" BECAME MY FAVORITE SONG

It was daunting going into a closed MRI at Smil Imaging after doctors found I had a rare form of cancer, orbital. In addition to having claustrophobia, I had to wear a mask to prevent my eyes from moving. Forty minutes in the tunnel with the accompanying banging noise without any music would be unbearable.

In that period, from 2008 to 2010, the only way to get music during such a procedure was to find a caring female radiologist—I avoided males at all costs. Luckily for me, I was allowed music, and my album of choice was *Eagles Greatest Hits*. When the MRI test ended, the power ballad being played was "Desperado," with lyrics by Glen Frey and Don Henley. (This song was the duo's first collaboration in 1973, and it appeared on the album *Desperado* as well as numerous compilation albums. It was also voted second most favorite Eagles song in a *Rolling Stone* magazine poll and was number 494 on the magazine's 2004 list of "The 500 Greatest Songs of All Time.")

STARBUCKS MANAGER OVER-WHELMED BY ORGANIC COFFEE USE

I had cancer on the tip of my pancreas, and an alternative-medicine doctor recommended a coffee enema. The caffeine in the coffee enema would avoid the stomach. I was game once I learned of a highly regarded practitioner who did colonics for cleansing and provided coffee enemas when requested. The spiritual and wonderfully caring Rosemarie would handle the procedure.

The office was located in Old Town, Scottsdale. The cost was eighty dollars, but I was required to bring the coffee, as there was no prescription. I'm not a coffee drinker, so Rosemarie advised bringing a quart of warm organic coffee. There was a Starbucks nearby on Main Street, so that's where I went.

Upon entering the Starbucks, I was greeted by the manager-barista, who informed me that they get few requests for organic, but that he could make an awesome cup. He was all smiles as he brought the coffee to the counter, waiting for me to taste it, hoping to be praised. I hated to tell him, but I had no choice, "Your organic coffee is going up my rectum."

The manager gave me a look of disbelief but recovered smartly, *and* he gave me a twenty-dollar gift card to Starbucks.

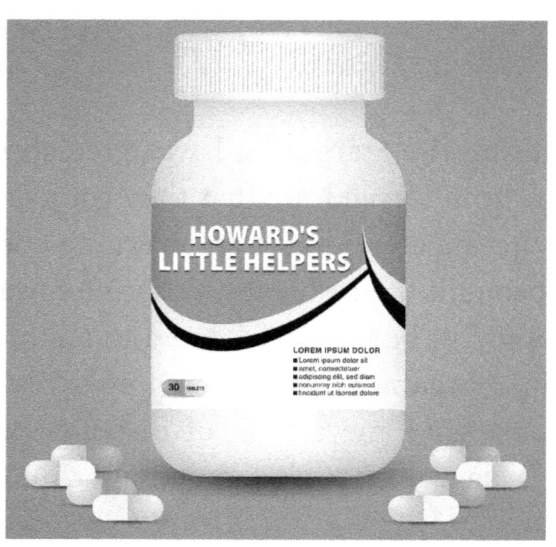

SHOCKING NEWS:
XANAX IS HABIT FORMING

My cancer result appeared in a blood test at age 48, the same age my father died. Needless to say, I was very concerned, as everyone told me I was just like Dad. To cure my sudden case of "high anxiety," an optometrist friend, Dr. Frank Spirn, made an appointment for me to visit a psychiatrist who was a colleague of his at a hospital in Edison, New Jersey.

I remember the drive to his office. I was barely able to stay on the road. The doctor recommended I take Xanax—a single pill—and all my troubles would go away.

He was 100 percent correct—I never felt better in my life. Shortly thereafter, though, anxiety returned, but I have stayed with a minor dose of Xanax for thirty-five years. It's a cheap prescription drug—a controlled substance with no visible side effects. Even if it's nothing more than a placebo, who cares.

When I first went on Xanax, I felt I needed to tell my mother, who was living in Miami Beach. She said it was no big deal—everyone in Florida was on Xanax.

Recently, I went to Walgreens for the first time due to a move—I'd always been a CVS customer. The pharmacist there informed me Xanax can be habit forming. I laughed and paid him six dollars for sixty pills. I take two a day, which is a very modest dose. The very gifted therapist Dr. Frank P., after many sessions, told me I was incorrectly diagnosed as being clinically depressed, but still said that for anxiety, nothing better than this drug.

MOP NOT NEEDED

A major part of becoming cancer free, in addition to more chemotherapy, was the lifestyle change, most specifically, becoming a vegan, which is much more restrictive than becoming a vegetarian. The alternative medical doctor whose care I was under was Dr. Ronald Peters of Mind, Body, Medicine. Peters had started out as a public health doctor after graduating from UCLA.

In his book, a required reading for his patients, he says, "Exploring the Psychology of Disease, the case is strongly made that while the West is far ahead of the East in emergency care, when it comes to preventive care, the West is far behind the East." To make this point, Peters asks the question, What should be done if you go into a flooded room? In the West, you would be advised take out a mop; in the East, you would turn off the faucet.

A vegan (which I was religiously for years) is an individual who doesn't eat anything that has a parent or that falls from the sky, which rules out meat, chicken, fish, fruits, and dairy. Geri and I argue over no fruits, but Peters is firm on the subject; the body can't distinguish between sugar from the fruit and sugar from processed foods.

Once I reached eighty, I became a cheating vegan, becoming more sociable and adding to my diet: sushi, skinless grilled chicken, and (when no one is looking) a slice of key lime pie. This reminds me of the woman mentioned in *Chicken Soup for the Soul*, which I read when I was much younger. Author Jack Canfield tells the story of a woman who when turning eighty said if she could live life over again, she eat more ice cream.

LAST PERSON TO TELL?
YOUR WIFE...

For a brief period, I was under the psychiatric care of Ron Sorvino (actor Paul Sorvino's brother, who recently died); both looked very much alike. Paul was highly regarded in the profession, at a time when psychiatrists not only dispensed drugs but provided therapy. The problem was that Paul worked too many hours, and on more than one occasion, with his head down and writing, he would fall asleep.

Paul also ran a therapy group that I attended. The rule of the game: you couldn't leave the group without unanimous member permission.

The turning point for my departure was when a group member advised me that as he was having sex with his wife, he fantasized about a female golf pro at the nearby United States Golf Association (USGA) facility. The patient felt so guilty that he couldn't work or sleep and needed to tell his wife to clear his conscience.

Paul—we all used first names, no last names—said the last person to tell would be your wife. Thinking with no action is understandable but harmless, and in time the golf pro would fade away. It was common sense advice, but I expected more from the profession.

The wonderful staff at Pinnacle Peak Dental Care.

THE ONLY PERSON I EVER THOUGHT ABOUT MURDERING WAS MY ORTHODONTIST

Getting braces at a young age seemed very much like a right-of-passage. Everyone I knew was getting braces, and the discussions were always about retainers at night, rubber bands, and how long you would have to wear them.

I was given no choice. The doctor selected for me was Harry Zeitels, whose office was always filled; he never made his appointment times. The first step in the process was to take an impression of the teeth using a smelly compound that hardened quickly. Dr. Zeitels jammed the loaded fixture into my mouth, closed my mouth, told me not to move and that he would be back shortly.

The problem: Zeitels forgot about me—too many patients to manage—and I was there for several hours, while the compound hardened to a point that removing it would require a pair of pliers and elephant-like strength. The pain was extreme, and finally the problem was solved. Off went the dentist, without a word of apology; he had no time for pleasantries with a full office. I believed he deserved to be murdered, and my defense would be youth, neglect, and his inflicting pain with no regard.

Today, I visit Pinnacle Peak Dental Care in Scottsdale, an office full of pleasant and talented ladies, headed by the talented wife and husband team of Jordyn and Taylor Hollingsworth. The care is flawless and, unlike the early days, painless. Pam, their dental hygienist, like so many before, complains my tongue is always in the way; I explain that the tongue is an independent entity with a mind of its own, there to protect me from outside forces.

However, you can't get too excited about the progress in painless dentistry, as the pain now comes when you pay the bill: the so-called treatment plan. Believe it or not, a single crown is in the $1,200 to $1,500 range, and feasible insurance is usually not available. In short, I would still murder Zeitels; and as for Pinnacle Peak, I would float a loan.

CARDINALS STADIUM NOT FOR FOOTBALL BUT FOR COVID-19

I have been going to NFL games since the early 1950s. I am pleased to share that I attended *The Greatest Game Every Played* when my NY Giants lost to the Baltimore Colts in sudden death overtime at Yankee Stadium. I also sat in the stands at the Los Angeles Coliseum to watch the first two Super Bowls, before sparse crowds. Bob Hope even sat in a row directly in front of me once.

Today, I would love to watch the Arizona Cardinals play, but frankly, it's too expensive and time consuming. And, more importantly, I only root for the Giants.

One funny thing happened recently: I had an appointment at the State Farm Stadium, not to see the hometown Cardinals play, but to get my first COVID-19 vaccine. We drove around the parking lot in Disney-like fashion and when we finally got to the last station, without getting out of the car, Geri (who was driving) got poked in the left arm, and at the same time I was poked in the right.

Getting the shot was a piece of cake, but getting an appointment online required CIA assistance. We celebrated by going out to lunch at Pita Jungle in Desert Ridge, our favorite spot for a delicious, affordable, and healthy meal. The good news: unlike the Cardinals, who are just so-so, we had no side effects and have not gotten COVID to date, having taken a second shot also at the ballpark and one booster.

BEYOND COMPREHENSION:
DOCTORS GET SICK

Mother lamented that as she aged, outliving her doctors became a reality. I smiled when she discussed how difficult it was to break-in new doctors. Mother had moved from North Miami Beach to Boca Raton at this point.

Today, as I reside in Cave Creek, Arizona, having recently turned eighty-three years young, many of my doctors are happily still alive, but a few have retired and moved. Oncologist Michael Roberts and urologist Robert Shapiro—who played the Michigan fight song while measuring my prostate—retired largely as a result of changes in how medical care is provided.

The close personal relationship between doctors and their patients is largely a relic of the past. Sadly, organizations they worked for and built have been gobbled up by large healthcare organizations like Honor Health.

My personal care physician, Robert Prier, a much younger doctor, left for Bend, Oregon, because at Honor Health he was limited to seeing patients only two days a week. He had to balance his time with administrative duties because he had become a medical director.

I am delighted to report that new my hematologist and oncologist, John Bibb, is a breath of fresh air for me; it took me months to see him, as he was totally booked and not seeing new patients. I found out Bibb was a big baseball fan and brought him my recent publication *Saving Baseball* and used my wits to work my way in to his practice. Bibb is the perfect age for a doctor: early fifties, which is young enough to be current, but old enough to have seen a good number of patients.

Dr. "Please call me John" Bibb is unique—he gives you a welcoming hug to establish an immediate connection and show he cares, so you don't feel like you're just a number. Unlike most oncologists, he is concerned about total health, not just cancer. Dr. Bibb's small team, including NP Josie Pirie, herself a breast cancer survivor, have all bought in on this. They're also a fun group. On Halloween, as you can see in the photo on the previous page, they all wore Where's Waldo shirts, including the doctors.

*"Everyone thinks
they have the best dog,
and none of them are wrong."*

MAN'S BEST FRIEND

I have always loved dogs, ever since the first time I saw the 1943 MGM movie *Lassie Come Home*. I grew up in Parkchester, a planned high-rise apartment community in Da Bronx of approximately 40,000 individuals. The owners, Metropolitan Life, delivered on a visionary concept that had but two deficiencies: no air-conditioning and no four-legged pets. We did what most everyone else did, filling the void with turtles, goldfish, and parakeets.

By contrast, Dad had a collie that was killed by an automobile picking up the morning paper, and he raised carrier pigeons on the roof, attaching a message to their legs and sending the pigeons to deliver the messages. It's little wonder that as married adults, getting a dog was a top priority for me and Geri, who was also a product of Parkchester—having children was several years away for us.

We've had five dogs in total. They were all wonderful pets—and four of which lived long lives as measured in dog years. Number one was Tiffany, a miniature short-haired Dachshund; number two, Josephine, a short haired Dachshund; number three, Charlie, a yellow Labrador; number four, Tewskie (short for the town of Tewksbury, where he was rescued), a Labrador mix who always found comfort under the coffee table; number five, Scooter, a short-haired miniature male Dachshund; and our current pet, named after Yankees shortstop Phil Rizzuto, and a ballplayer in his own right.

Putting a dying dog down, while humane, is an awful experience; but in time, we move on, recognizing we need "man's best friend" (a quote incorrectly attributed to comedian Groucho Marx) in our lives.

We began dog ownership by looking for AKC registration, but over time, rescuing a dog became paramount. There is also a growing consensus that rescued dogs live longer. One of the thrills of my life was having breakfast at the New Yorker Hotel across from Madison Square Garden the morning after conclusion of the Westminster Kennel Club Dog Show. The show brought together 20 breeds representing 3,500 dogs, and many of the dogs were in the hotel lobby for checkout; viewing all these pure breeds was a sight to behold.

MOVING TO SIBERIA
WITHOUT OUR BEST FRIEND

We drove down from Norwood to Whitman, Massachusetts, to select our first dog. We were hoping to get the first pup, and left the owner with a littler four remaining. We selected the female because we'd heard they were easier to paper train, and named her Tiffany, after the prestigious Fifth Avenue jewelry store. Tiffany sat on Geri's lap in the car. She was so tiny, and she gave the car that wonderful new puppy odor.

We both worked, so the dog was confined to the kitchen during the day. Geri came home first from teaching elementary school at the John Nixon school in Sudbury. Tiffany never barked and had a habit of walking around our area rug to get to the sliding window doors. The only bad thing she ever did was pee on a set of commercial storyboards left on the floor.

Tiffany joined us when we moved to LA, and we watched her grow old gracefully, though she lost her vision. Later, I accepted a job offer in New Jersey, and it took me days to tell the family, as back in the '70s no one left LA for Siberia, New Jersey.

Tiffany was in the bedroom as I bravely told Geri and our two kids, Lauren and Michael, the news—they were not happy.

The following morning, we found Tiffany had crossed the rainbow bridge. Dogs do have a special sense of when bad things are coming.

JOSEPHINE BECOMES SHERLOCK HOLMES

O ur five-bedroom home with basement and pool, in Westfield, New Jersey, was the party house for Michael when he was in high school. He assured us that everyone, including girls, behaved. He sold us a bill of goods saying that, among other things, we didn't need to worry about him drinking and driving. Thankfully, the only dangerous thing the boys did was jump off the singer sewing machine rail, high atop the pool equipment, into the pool.

In the winter, the kids played hockey on the ice above the pool cover. Geri and I always went out on party night, and upon reaching the driveway, we made noise alerting party-goers we were home. Once we were inside, the kids would gather around, smiling and telling us how much they appreciated partying at 100 Winchester Way.

Josephine was a wonderful pet. When we moved from a ranch to a classic two-floor colonial, she learned (without teaching) to climb the stairs on a diagonal. My daughter's lab, Hannah, by contrast, had to be carried to the second floor where the sleeping quarters were.

Josephine did have one special moment on a warm late spring day the morning following a party and sleepover. As she sat squatted down to do her business by the pool, out came a soiled condom, evidence that our son lied about sexual activity.

Michael was upstairs and I called up to him, asking him to come down to the pool immediately. I asked the standard question, "There was no fooling around with the girls last night, was there?" Michael said of course not. Then, I showed him the condom and explained how it came to be in my possession. Beyond his turning red, I don't remember what his punishment was, but he was clearly on notice.

THE RIDE FROM HELL

Josephine was on her last legs when Lauren was attending NYU Law and living in the East Village. She came across a fellow student who decided what was best for his puppy was to find a good suburban home. Lauren suggested her mom and I adopt him, and we agreed. So, we had a rendezvous in Washington Square Park to pick up the pup.

Lauren arrived with the puppy, Charlie, but to our peril he weighed over sixty pounds and had never been in an automobile. Our car, a four door Honda Civic, was just big enough for the forty-five minute trip to Westfield, New Jersey. I drove while Geri held on for dear life.

Geri dubbed this "The Ride from Hell." Once home, we somehow managed to get Charlie into our partially finished basement. We closed the door, hoping for the best, but suspecting the basement would be ruined by morning. It was.

We were ill-suited as parents for a large dog. We soon learned we needed a large crate and a trainer. It was weeks—maybe a month—before Charlie was allowed to roam freely in the house and our large-fenced backyard, centered by a covered pool. Although we fed Charlie diet dog chow, he still grew to be 110 pounds. He was magnificent to look at and became (as everyone said) a life-sized member of the family.

I have so many wonderful memories of Charlie: he sat erect in the passenger seat allowing me to drive in the HOV lane; he beat me regularly in a game of hide and seek; he was a Lab, but because of a near-drowning incident—he got trapped on the pool cover—he was afraid to go on the ocean at the Jersey Shore. He also slept with my wife when I had two long consulting gigs in Texas, and I started calling him the "Big White Stallion."

There was also the time we thought we picked him up at the kennel, but instead we were given the wrong Lab—a fatter and a female. At a play date with a group of dogs and their owners, he swallowed their toy treats, and he ran on the clay tennis courts at Netherwood Tennis Club in NJ, never touching a net or line.

PART TWO

ELBOW GREASE

Elbow grease;
the kind that won't soil a shirt.
— Gary Moore

General Douglas MacArthur

SECTION 5

PATRIOTIC DUTY

I can't remember a time when I was not patriotic and not a strong supporter of US military. Dad was part of "The Greatest Generation," having served in the Navy as a signalman on *Doyle C. Barnes*, a destroyer escort. Dad was drafted in 1943, one day before his thirty-fifth birthday. He was married and a father, and if he had made it to thirty-five, he would have never served. When he returned home from service, I ran away because he had grown a mustache. After the war, Dad took me to the Chrysler Building, where the lobby was filled with US military armor; a nice soldier allowed me to climb to the top of the tank.

Years later, on April 20, 1951, one of my heroes, General Douglas MacArthur, whom my Dad served under in the Pacific, was given a NYC Ticker-Tape Parade, and played hooky from P.S. 102 with parental approval. His words before a joint session of Congress for his Farewell Address to the nation still stays with me; he ended by quoting the famous phrase, "Old soldiers never die—they just fade away."

I'm a big sports fan, but when I hear the words NFL draft, I instead think about the year I turned eighteen, the age when registering for the draft is required by law. I never thought about fleeing across the Canadian border, which really didn't become fashionable until Vietnam. To register, you spent the day at 39 Whitehall Station waiting to pass the physical. The needles were long and painful, and the same Army medics seemed to follow you from floor to floor. I was proud to pass the exam, and my draft card arrived in the mail shortly thereafter.

Once drafted, there were many options to serve. I selected six months of active duty and five-and-a-half years reserve time, consisting of one night a week and two weeks of summer camp. As a reservist, you could be activated in case of a national emergency, but that seemed highly unlikely at the time. Advantages of this program: no interruption of civilian life, along with graduate school, marriage, children, and a career.

I was attending NYU in Greenwich village at the time, adjacent to Washington Square Park. On any given day, between classes, you could play a game of chess with a homeless person drinking booze in a small brown bag and get your ass kicked.

I joined the reserve outfit in nearby Sheridan Square. The unit was the 312th Base Post Office, and our mission twas to operate a post office at the European Theatre during the war. This certainly didn't seem like an essential mission to all us college kids, and because of this we had a hard time staying awake during our weekly Thursday nigh meetings that were led by reserve personnel who were career postal employees.

I learned precious little at those meetings. But, if the meetings ended early enough and if the subway connections were good, I could arrive home in time to watch Robert Stack as Eliot Ness, star of *The Untouchables*. It was the first great crime series after *Dragnet*, which featured Jack Webb as Joe Friday. He wore badge number 714, Webb's tribute to his idol, Babe Ruth.

There was nothing much to learn about posting mail, and I fought like hell to stay awake. The most curious thing was a mimeographed sheet of instructions on what to do in case of an atomic attack. The instructions simply said, "Leave home and arrive immediately at Camp Drum in Watertown, New York. That was 331 miles away —five hours and 37 minutes by auto." Naturally, there was no mention of one minor detail: what to do if the bombs started dropping before reaching the targeted Camp Drum destination.

FLYING TEN: A FITTING WAY TO START BASIC TRAINING

I arrived at Fort Dix, New Jersey, near Wrightstown, a miserable and remote place, on January 29, 1961, after receiving my BS Degree from NYU. It was in the middle of a cold winter, and the Third Training Regiment was the furthest thing from the PX, or general store, and our only encounter with the real world. Basic training lasted eight weeks, and each week seemed like an eternity; you were so envious of any soldier who was much further along.

After the bus ride from the Port Authority terminal, we arrived at base central to receive clothing: a duffel bag, a belt, a name tag, a cap with woolen flaps, a pair of gloves, shirts, pants, socks, boots (if they were brown you were screwed, as the Army had just gone to black, so you had to paint them black); I don't remember if there was underwear.

Each soldier received ten bucks to hold them over until the first payroll period. At the end of the line was a mean-looking son of a bitch, the E8 Master Sergeant who, as we were to learn, had total responsibility and control to turn us into infantrymen. He had a deserved reputation of hating college kids.

In front of the sergeant was a desk sign that said, "Give to the Sergeant's Relief Fund, $10 contribution required." There was also a list of those who gave and those who didn't—not a single smart college kid refused to give. It was appropriately called "The Flying Ten" because first, it was in your hands, then it flew away.

NOTHING WORSE THAN BEING RECYCLED DURING BASIC

I was shocked when my Mother brought a date with her when she visited me at Fort Dix. This was a first for her. I saw her companion as a possible replacement for my dad, and I was understandably prepared to dislike him.

Even though I didn't like him, this guy did have certain things going for him including being a college graduate and he was an accomplished ice skater—he and mom skated at Rockefeller Center. He also owned a clothing store in the Flatbush section of Brooklyn. Unfortunately for him, he was also very unappealing looking. Much to my relief, he didn't pass muster and my mother moved on from him pretty quickly.

One day, Mom noticed my face appeared healthy, but bright red. She guessed this meant I was getting too much sun. I thought nothing of it.

When I awakened next morning, I noticed a rash on my stomach. The medical officer was making his morning rounds, so I called the rash to his attention. The officer commanded me to drop my drawers, which I did, and he said I had Scarlet Fever.

Upon this diagnosis, I thought I was going to die. I didn't realize that though scarlet fever was once an infectious disease in the 1800s, it was now curable through a combination of antibiotics and a week of isolation. Then the bad news hit: I would have to take basic over—I was to be recycled! This was the word no recruit ever wanted to hear.

This was most frustrating, especially when my former training buddies were all moving toward graduation. They laughed their asses off when they found out what was going to happen.

During basic, I experienced a handful of once-in-a-lifetime moments. These included sneezing after putting on my gas mask in a night drill and then running in to a tree; volunteering to type (I had been a Kelly Girl) and then jogging a mile holding a typewriter over my head; and by mistake, leaving William Shirer's *The Rise and Fall of the Third Reich* on the foot of my bed—a horrible mistake during an inspection.

The bed needed to have perfect hospital corners, and a tight fit so that a quarter could bounce off the blanket to pass inspection. I thought I'd passed, but the sergeant noticed the book, and maybe assuming I was a Nazi sympathizer, tipped the bed over. For a week, I had to make every bed in my bunk.

On the day I left Ft. Dix, after completing a six months tour, the *Army Times* page-one headline read "All Reservists Extended." The sergeant shook my hand as I departed with the *Army Times* in hand. "I can't wait to get you back to train you for combat in the jungles of Vietnam," he said.

Fifty plus years later, my two grandsons, Henry Eisen and James Michael Peretz, played soccer on the Ft. Dix soccer fields.

VIETNAM WAR RESERVIST ANXIETY

August 25, 1961, I recall like it was yesterday. I was driving south on the FDR Drive in Manhattan to attend class at NYU where I was a Graduate Research Assistant. As a result of political pressure, selected Army Reserve units were being activated. The units going were announced on the car radio, and I was scared to death, hence my zig-zag driving. Remember, I was in the 312th, and the units activated that evening included the 324th, 325th, 310A, 372aD, 380th, and 372 AD.

Frank L., a fellow research assistant, wasn't as lucky. His unit's mission was to repair boots—they were cobblers, hardly critical to the war effort. They complained loudly, and the last I ever heard from Frank, their individual missions were changed, and off he went to Jump School at Ft. Bragg.

I had yet to attend summer camp as I was on a management training program requiring me to move every eight weeks. I properly notified the Army after each move, but they never caught up with me. Once the training was over, I landed permanently in Boston, and one of the managers was Tommy Thompson, a full-bird colonel in the Air Force Reserves at the AF Recovery Group. I was able to transfer there. I knew the colonel to be a really good person, and I preferred one weekend a month at the Boston Navy Yard to one night weekly.

On August 7, 1964, the Gulf of Tonkin Incident happened, where North Vietnam warships attacked the USS *Maddox* and the USSC *Turner*. President Johnson went on the air to announce the seriousness of this escalation. The following Saturday morning was our scheduled reserve meeting, and Colonel Thompson addressed the group, saying we were all on alert to be activated but would be allowed to call home on Sunday night to advise our loved ones of our orders.

I had just gotten married on February 1, 1962, and was worried I wouldn't see my wife again. Turns out, this was a drill. There was no deployment and we went home as scheduled.

I attended three AF two-week summer camps to complete my six-year obligation. The first camp I attended was at the Grenier Air Force Base in Manchester, New Hampshire. It was an SAC (Strategic Air Command) base. The SAC flight line was most impressive, with rows of fueled jets as far as the eye could see. There was also an armed soldier at parade rest with a rifle and a German Shepherd at his side in front of each aircraft. SAC was the brainchild of General Curtis LeMay, and all of his planes were loaded with atomic bombs. Half of the planes were required to be in the air at all times. One nice gesture by Col. Thompson was that he flew us all back to Boston in an AF Cargo Aircraft.

The remaining two summer camps were spent at Otis Air Force Base on Cape Cod. Imagine that, summering on the Cape. On the last day of military service, I loaded up at the PX with low prices and no taxes, then I stepped on the gas pedal, radio blasting, and crossed the Bourne Bridge. I sincerely hoped my military service would be behind me. I would have one more close call to being a soldier again, but luckily they ended up not enlisting in officer candidate school.

While I was never gung-ho about the service. I was proud to serve and would have gone in to combat if called, but it wasn't my thing. While an all-volunteer military force is a good thing, in my opinion, the country would be better served if all eighteen-year-olds were required to do a minimum of two years of government service.

Tom Hanks

DID WORLD WAR II
REALLY HAPPEN

In 1999, my Houston-based toy client, DSI, introduced Blockman, designed by the wonderfully talented Barry Stiles. The product combined Lego™-styled construction blocks; Lego™ patents had run their course, with poseable action figures. I was a huge supporter of the product line dating back to my GI Joe™ days.

At the 1999 toy show, we built a huge diorama demonstrating a typical World War II action scene. I was taking a young female reporter with trade press credentials on a showroom tour. Blockman was our number-one introduction, so I asked her, "What do you know about WWII?"

She remarked, in a serious tone, "Wasn't that the war Tom Hanks was in?"

Of course, Hanks did star in the 1998 film *Saving Private Ryan*, which dealt with the D-Day invasion and was nominated for eleven Academy Awards, but I was astonished that this was the only thing this young woman knew about this historical event that had such a huge impact worldwide and took so many lives.

One of my biggest pet peeves is that American history is no longer a mandatory course in our schools. Maybe "The Greatest Generation" will likewise vanish from the public's collective memory soon too.

"Don't let the fear of striking out hold you back."

— Babe Ruth

MONOGRAM STAMPED ON OUR FOREHEADS

After receiving MBA Honors from NYU, while also serving as a research assistant I set my sights on one job: research account executive at Young & Rubicam, a leading advertising agency during the Mad Men era. Unlike other agencies where account executive types started in the mailroom, at Y&R I would be a Research Account Executive.

Two individuals were selected for these plum positions. I was in the final four, but I never had a chance. The Chairman of the Board (COB) went to Stanford and selected a Stanford graduate, and the president, who went to Dartmouth, chose a Dartmouth alum.

After that disappointment, I turned my attention to the CIA, where the starting salary for a GS9 was well above going rate for a private industry job. A CIA position also came with many perks like sending me to Harvard for Russian Studies, early retirement with full benefits (if you passed on personal and vacation time), accumulated sick leave, and never having to take work home because of security concerns.

After passing Navy security clearance, including a polygraph, I was told one of my heroes, JFK, would read my reports. The first assignment was to become the free world expert on the mining of tin in Manchuria, which I found less than inspiring, so I passed on this opportunity.

A big break came when I was selected for the GE MBA Marketing Training Program by Jim Squires, who worked out of the GE Building at 570 Lexington Avenue. Twenty-four trainees were recruited per year, two per month. Training assignments at different GE facilities lasted eight weeks, and each location came with a furnished apartment.

The pitch was that we were to be the future executives of the company. Once a year, all trainees attended a meeting where we heard impressive executives talk about the future. One presentation has stuck with me all these years: it was delivered, per usual, on mounted lined graph paper by J. B. McKittrick of corporate research.

The lecture topic was "The Real Japanese Pearl Harbor" and featured six transistor radios being retailed at less than GE's product cost; secondarily, we were leaving the photo flash business to Sylvania, as flash bulbs would no longer be needed; and lastly, a discussion of product planning, a new discipline being rolled out.

The shocking part was the twenty-four of us all looked and smelled alike, although I stood out in a brown (not gray) suit. We also had similar experiences as we traveled the GE circuit. Unique to the program was that when you graduated, there were no jobs waiting and you had to arrange for interviews and sell yourself.

Taking the GE offer caused me to break my first promise to Geri: we would never leave the Big Apple.

EVERY SEVENTH FRIDAY
IT'S IRMA LUCERELLI TIME

Irma Lucerelli, aide to Jim Squires, was in effect the travel agent for us GE trainees. We called in every seventh Friday, not having a clue where we would be going next, apart from knowing where all the GE locations were. First stop: a private home at 16 Taconic Street in Pittsfield, Massachusetts, working for Dick Harris of the Chemical Materials Department.

It was an exciting time as Lexan, a new polycarbonate plastic—the hardest plastic known to mankind—was being introduced to the trades by reader response. My job was to track and organize coupons. Surprising to all was the number-one application for this new wonder plastic: outdoor bubble gum machines.

From there, we moved on to the Park Lee Alice Apartments on the West side of Phoenix. GE had recently entered the large-frame computer business, since we were the largest computer purchaser following the federal government, and the largest employer of electrical engineers. This business failed partially because Phoenix was too far from customers, and mostly because the weather was nice and there was so much to do outside, the engineers who formerly worked into the wee hours each day left promptly at 5 p.m. to explore the outdoors. We had such a good time in the Valley of the Sun.

I remember dining on a one-of-a-kind, never duplicated blue cheese burger there that had the blue cheese melted in the middle. This was a delicious first at Romley's, which is sadly no longer in business.

On our first wedding anniversary at Mountain Shadows, we saw Ted Williams at the bar, then we played tennis at night in Encanto Park, where you needed quarters to keep the lights on. We left tennis to drive north to watch the snow fall but turned around because it was freaking cold! On regular weekdays, we sat poolside, mostly by ourselves, when the weather report indicated high cloudiness.

Next on the itinerary was Cicero, Illinois, outside of the Chicago headquarters of GE's Hotpoint Appliance Division. It was most fascinating watching them tear down competitors' appliances to their cores to perform value engineering.

We stayed at the Oak Park Chateau, the only hotel on the program. On our first Sunday in town, there was a mafia funeral at the local cemetery. It's not a legend that police stayed away as competing mafia families came to pay their respects.

Geri worked to stay busy, lying about her length of stay. The funniest moment came when she was a clinic coordinator at St. Luke's Presbyterian Hospital and she requested a patient bring in a stool sample. The patient arrived the following day, not with a stool but a bowl of homemade stew.

In Schenectady, New York, the most GE of all towns, we stayed at the Netherlands Village apartments. We found a NYC-style deli, Braverman's, and traveled to Saratoga, the town made famous by author Edna Ferber in her 1941 work *Saratoga Trunk*. Work was located at the Advanced Technology Laboratories (ATL), where I was totally in over my head.

There was a report that was to be made about cryogenics by a PhD in physics. He was scheduled to deliver his big report to upper management, but he showed up an hour late. The funny/not so funny thing was, it was daylight savings time and he had moved his clock back instead of forward. This was considered so dumb that he was subsequently fired.

NYC was the last destination where I worked on contracts for International General Electric. We stayed at the London Terrace Apartment on West 23rd Street, which covered the entire block. Imagine a swimming pool on the first floor and a supermarket on premise.

After graduation, there was an opening in the Major Appliance Division at the New England branch in Cambridge, which I accepted. Their offices was adjacent to the Charles River and near Harvard Square. We found an apartment on Chiswick Road below Cleveland Circle. I protested but eventually agreed with Geri's decision that a dishwasher was more important than a bedroom.

She found a job teaching elementary school at the John Nixon School in the quaint town of Sudbury, and she loved everything about her work. We celebrated my new job by going to the Jacob Worth Tavern to have a yard of ale.

GERI TELLS THE TRUTH, ALMOST ENDS MY CAREER JUST AS IT STARTS

My first day of work began with Geri and me being greeted by "Woody" Wilson. He had a reputation for hating trainees, but he was always fulfilled the minimum obligation of training people to become GE's "executives of the future."

One hurdle to achieving this was that you had to start your career as a sales counselor. There were many stories of Harvard MBA trainees not making it out of the field because of this. Woody preferred his sales force to be composed of lifelong New Englanders who were hungry because they had large families and big mortgages.

"Woody," nicknamed for President Woodrow Wilson, was nearing retirement age by this time. Even though he was wealthy from all the GE stock he owned, we all ended up chipping in to buy him a Cadillac as his retirement gift.

We entered Woody's wood-paneled power office with its spectacular view of the Charles River, and at that moment the Harvard crew was out there practicing rowing. Woody greeted us warmly, shaking our hands and making polite conversation.

This was a bit painful, because he unfortunately had a bad case of stuttering. He struggled to ask Geri what she did for a living, and Geri, who majored in speech at Queens College, calmly replied, "I'm a speech therapist." Going forward, I made certain to avoid eye contact with him.

President John Fitzgerald Kennedy

DRIVING AROUND BEANTOWN, I GOT A STRANGE SENSE OF SILENCE

My sales territory was Route 9 from Boston to Worcester. I sold white goods, appliances, and brown goods, televisions and stereos to franchise GE dealers. I did step out of the box to win a sales contest, taking the first television set in the industry (eleven-inch black and white) to retail for just under $100 ($99.95).

The sale was to a dress shop, which was hardly a qualifying franchised dealer. The shop owner, affectionately referred to as "City Jake," sold the portable out the back door for just a $5 profit, ignoring acceptable profit margins.

Corporate pencil pushers decided on the type of auto the sales force would have, and mine was no exception. It was a stick shift that I had to learn how to drive. I drove out of the lot with my head down so I could concentrate. This was no frills for sure. There was no radio, and instead of snow tires, I had chains and a bucket of sand.

On a crisp fall day in November 1963, as I was driving to my next sales call, it seemed the city was asleep but it was daytime. With no car radio, I had no idea what was going on and decided to drive to our Cambridge office. Upon climbing the stairs to the lobby, I observed everyone crying.

What was going on? I thought maybe a world war had started, but I was wrong. On November 22, 1963, President John Fitzgerald Kennedy was assassinated. JFK was Boston's very own and the first Catholic to become President.

The next week, I was glued to the television, as we all mourned JFK during the funeral led by Cardinal Richard James Cushing, the Archbishop of Boston. Cushing, in his distinctive Irish brogue, delivered the eulogy. Cushing famously said, "Plan ahead: it wasn't raining when Noah built his ark."

"Parents didn't feel uneasy about buying GI Joe™. They considered GI Joe™ to be a surrogate father or a big brother or a hero."

—Donald Levine

A close colleague of mine was Hasbro's chief of research and development when the toy debuted and he was known as the "father of GI Joe™"

SECTION 7

GI JOE™ TO THE RESCUE!

Leaving General Electric for Hassenfeld Bros. was an easy decision. Mainly because I wouldn't have to relocate. At GE, the key to success was to find a manager who was moving-up the ladder and have him take you along. That would, however, require a move every time you wanted a promotion.

At Hassenfeld Bros., the heir apparent was Stephen Hassenfeld, third generation who was just three years younger than me, and I would be reporting directly to him. As the story goes, Stephen left John Hopkins early to help in the growing family business. In time, we would find out this was a cover story.

Further, GI Joe had been launched just a year earlier. This tiny company was best known for Mr. Potato Head, which was introduced in 1953. Steve's father, Merrill, made a bad deal— he agreed to pay a royalty rather than a $2,500 cash buyout, and was now on a fast track, so my marketing skill set would be required. I was to become a marketing department of one.

It was a shock to leave the fourth largest company in the US, GE, to work for a tiny, family-owned enterprise, where almost every manager was somehow related to the Hassenfelds. Everyone was also Jewish, which was indescribable.

This can best be illustrated when I went to see Charlie Oldbaum in accounting to get paid. I had never met him. I was on the executive payroll, which meant hand checks, and he was the paymaster.

I walked into his office and introduced myself. He looked up and asked how old I was. I replied twenty-six, and he said that I was being paid too much money for someone so young. My reflex response was: I'm Jewish. The check immediately went from his hand to mine. This was the first time I had ever used the Jewish card to my advantage.

I learned that all the affluent Jewish people in town lived on the East Side of Providence, Rhode Island. Our company was in nearby Pawtucket, and I resided in Norwood, Massachusetts. I was happy to be living in a south Boston suburb, content to be far away from the craziness.

I loved the excitement of the toy business where it was all about new, hit products. Once a year, in March, the Annual Toy Fair was held in the Toy Building at 200 Fifth Avenue in NYC. Each manufacturer introduced their lines at th is time.

It was a big deal and everything was hush-hush before the show. Showroom windows were covered and employees hid everything. Conversing with the competition was like colluding with the enemy and was a definite no-no.

Once the show started, everyone ran around trying to learn what the other guy was doing, but getting into a competitor's showroom was a difficult feat. Word, however, would eventually begin to trickle out. Product ads in the three toy trade magazines were in the lobby, plus there was a lot of eavesdropping on conversations in crowded elevators, bathrooms and coffee shops. The spies were everywhere.

Soon there was buzz throughout the show, and almost immediately, you learned whether the upcoming business year was going to be good or bad. It was much like an opening for a Broadway show. People in the know on these first days ran to their stock brokers post haste.

My family—me, Geri, Lauren, and Tiffany—moved into the city weeks in advance to get the showrooms, catalogs, etc. ready for prime time. On a Saturday afternoon, a group of us from Hasbro went to the NYAC to shoot hoops, and to our surprise, so did a group from Mattel. The rumor was that Barbie was going to talk for the first time, and we all knew our big news: GI Joe talked. We considered the idea that the losing team would have to spill the beans on their project, but it was rejected as being too risky.

As to the mechanics of Talking GI Joe, he talked via a color-coded pull string mechanism. We had two working prototypes, each prone to failing. Our showroom table was draped, and on the floor under the table was John Hein, our Director of Engineering. He quietly kept us in business.

Worth noting, Barbie didn't talk and never has. Talking GI Joe was a dismal failure, never making it out of the Toy Show. The idea was a casualty of war. This was the reason boys played with "Joe" as a toy soldier. "Fighting Man from Head-to-Toe" and a talking "Joe" would be viewed as a doll, which was the kiss of death for an action figure.

First female Israeli ordnance officer of Beta Israel origin.

MORE NAZI'S NEEDED

The first meeting I recall was about an imbalance in GI Joe™ figure inventory. We had too many Brits and Aussies in-stock, and not enough Nazis. We had two options to consider: fly in more Nazi figures, or fly in Nazi uniforms to Rhode Island and change the uniforms of the slow-moving inventory.

I don't recall what we decided, but what is astonishing to me is that no one at the table, including myself, thought there was anything wrong with profiting from the sale of Nazi gear—it was just a routine business decision. Looking back, it is also interesting to note that all of the original figures were white. Trade consensus at that time, believe it or not, was that black children preferred to play with white dolls.

The Sears doll buyer, Ray Wagner, who would later become president of Mattel, was the largest customer in the business. He asked for a Negro GI Joe™, and Hasbro responded by creating one, but still used the same white body.

CEO Merrill Hassenfeld was influential in the United Jewish Appeal (UJA) and the Israeli Bond Drive. To raise money for Israel, there were periodic dinners where an important Jewish retail buyer was given an award. Manufacturers were required to take and pay for a table, and the individuals seated at the table were also called on personally donate as well. This was done by holding up fingers to correspond to the amount. To the novice, holding up two figures would mean $200, but in the "Machiavelli approach" to raising money for a worthwhile cause, two fingers meant $2,000!

To add authenticity, an Israeli soldier, frequently a woman in battle gear, would welcome guests and thank them at the end. Years later, Hasbro, which went public in 1968, was sited and fined by the SEC for acting on behalf of a foreign government—Israel.

MEETING KING HUSSEIN:
NO BIG DEAL

At the conclusion of the 1967's Six-Day War, won by Israel over their Arab neighbors, all parties came to the UN in NYC to look for a peaceful resolution. Somehow, both sides elected to stay at the Waldorf Towers, located next to the Waldorf Astoria. New York's finest patrolled on every floor for their security.

Stephen Hassenfeld resided at the Waldorf hotel while in the city. I was attending a meeting with him there when I realized I had left a report in my room at the Waldorf Towers, so in the middle of the afternoon I walked over and then took an elevator to my floor.

As I turned my metal key to enter my room, a big guy (he gets bigger every time I tell the story) came from behind, grabbed me, and knocked me down. I was startled but not hurt.

It turns out he was the bodyguard for King Hussein, the Constitutional Monarch of Jordan, and the King was told he had the entire floor to himself. The big guy escorted me to the end of the hallway to the plush Presidential Suite, where the five-foot-six king got up from his desk and shook my hand, he then apologized on behalf of his kingdom for my rough treatment at the hands of his bodyguard. I accepted his apology, went to my room, picked up the report, and went back to the meeting, telling no one of the incident.

I didn't ask for an autograph or a photo or financial compensation, and never thought about seeking legal representation for what happened. Back then, we didn't think that way. The King's apology was heart felt, he had pressing issues to deal with, and I had a meeting.

In 1994, King Hussein's country became only the second Arab state to recognize the State of Israel—Egypt's Anwar Sadat was the first, and he was later assassinated while in office.

JOHNNY CARSON APPEARANCE NOT WHAT WE HOPED

Hasbro's large doll entry in 1967 was called Little Miss No Name, and she had a lot going for her. She was designed by Deet D'Andrade and featured sad eyes inspired by Margaret Keane, whose work featured large-eyed children. The doll had permanently mussed hair, wore a burlap dress with a patch on it, had a plastic tear that attached through a hole under one of her eyes, and she was barefoot. She came in a box that made it look like she was walking through a snowstorm.

There were ads for the homeless doll that included text like: "She doesn't have a pretty dress. She doesn't have any shoes. She doesn't even have a home. All she has is love." (You can see original ads and hear the jingle on YouTube.) There was even a cross-promotion with Borden's Dutch Instant Chocolate Flavored Mix in 1968, and they created a catchy jingle for her.

After months of pursuit by PR Agent Walter Murphy, who would later insist that Geri and I have dinner with his client Rosemary Clooney at a NYC nightclub, Johnny Carson of *The Tonight Show* agreed to include the doll in his show's group of toys for the annual Christmas segment. This was a huge deal!

I sent out telegrams to all our accounts, advising them of the day and time the show would air. Stephen and I were in the audience when Johnny opened his sack of goodies and picked up Little Miss No Name. He immediately threw her aside, saying she was unappealing because she wasn't smiling.

Turns out Johnny was smarter than all of us. The doll was only in production for a few years. Oddly enough, collectors today are crazy for this doll. Prices for just the doll by itself are range from $275 to $500, and one in relatively rough condition with its original box recently sold on eBay for $1,850!

DOES THE
FLYING NUN DOLL FLY?

A new industry pioneering strategy was to promote low-priced toys in the first quarter rather than relying totally on Christmas. Hasbro had a full line of appropriately low-priced activity toys suitable for cold weather and indoor play. Many children received money for Christmas and Hasbro wanted it.

Their lead item this particular year was a licensed doll based upon the successful ABC sitcom *The Flying Nun*. This show first aired on September 7, 1967, and starred actress Sally Field in the title role of Sister Bertrille. (Field would go on to win all sorts of accolades, including Best Actress Academy Awards for both *Places in the Heart* and *Norma Ray.*)

I was given the assignment of traveling to Flint, Michigan, to assist Sam Schulman. He was an outside sales rep who handled several non-competing lines. Sam's number-one account was Yankee Stores, with twenty-one discount stores in southeastern Michigan. Sam was an old-time seller, relying on personality and close buyer relationships, rather than product knowledge and servicing. His signature look included always puffing on a lit cigar.

I went to a dinner with Sam, and was impressed when he stressed the importance of Yankee Stores maintaining a toy department in the first quarter, rather than showing them the product first. When Sam got around to showing his lead item, the Flying Nun, the show was a big success. But then the buyer asked if the Flying Nun doll could fly. Sam smiled and said, "Of course not, she is a doll!"

The buyer said, "When she flies, I'll consider ordering some."

The rest of presentation went downhill from there.

Side note about flying dolls: In 1994, Galoob Toys introduced Sky Dancers, a line of ballerina dolls that flew. They had foam wings, a launcher and a stand. Most of the industry thought the dolls wouldn't be able to pass the Consumer Product Safety Commission (CPSC) tests, but it took until the year 2000 before Sky Dancers were recalled.

Jack E. Leonard

Tina Louise

KNOCKOFFS, EVEN CLEVER ONES, RARELY WORK

Tie and Tangle was Hasbro's knockoff response to Bradley's Twister, the action game of the year in 1966, selling approximately three million copies. Instead of a plastic mat, with six rows of red circles and a spinner, we had a mat and long cord, and the person with the longest cord at the end was declared the winner. Like Bradley's Twister, the game Tie and Tangle was beat up in the press for "selling sex in a box." The commercial we created did much the same thing.

Our spot starred the very fat Jack E. Leonard, who pioneered "insult humor" before Don Rickles, and the beautiful

Tina Louise, best known for playing Ginger Grant in *Gilligan's Island*. Shooting the spot was a nightmare, because by the time the set was properly lit, Leonard was perspiring profusely and needed a break. When he was ready, Tina needed time off because her make up was running, and her beauty mark would be no longer covered.

After the commercial aired, I received a phone call from Sylvia Hassenfeld, Stephen's mother. She was a class act, and this was the first time we had spoken. Unfortunately, I was chewed out for promoting sex in that ad. (The only other encounter I had with Sylvia Hassenfeld was when I was preparing the company's first Annual Report and asked her to please forward her husband Merrill's favorite photo, which she did. When the report came out, Merrill was pissed off by his photo, saying it was unflattering. Of course, I refused to name his wife as the source.)

The Amazing Dunninger Game, like Tie and Tangle, was a knockoff of another Milton Bradley top-selling board game called Kreskin's ESP. It was named after The Amazing Kreskin, a television celebrity, though Kreskin claimed he was an entertainer, not a psychic.

Joseph Dunninger, world-renowned mentalist known as "The Amazing Dunninger," agreed to the licensing deal, and would do our commercial. He would also become the host of a local NYC live TV game show where studio guests would be interrogated.

The Sunday night before the commercial shoot, a group of us had dinner and "The Amazing Dunninger" was our guest. Geri joined us, and Dunninger's first words were directed at her. He claimed to have read her thoughts, saying she doubted his abilities. Geri admitted out loud to this being true.

Later, Dunninger gave me the Real Estate Section of the *NY Times*, asking me to cut out a single listing from the pages and place it in my jacket pocket. Dunninger truly was amazing—told me the listing in its entirety. We were now all believers, that is until the commercial shooting began the following morning.

The problem: Dunninger couldn't remember his lines. We ended up writing his lines on large poster sheets so he could read them off, much like they do for President Biden today. The first line was: "I am the Amazing Dunninger."

Both of our knockoff games failed in the marketplace, but Stephen got the last laugh when, in 1984, Hasbro purchased the Milton Bradley Company, manufacturer of both *Twister* and *Kreskin* games.

THE CALLAHAN TUNNEL FINGER

I was in Chicago to attend the three-day Hobby Show in the middle of January, and it was freezing, with wind chills close to 30 degrees below zero. Further, the show was at the Sherman Hotel, known for its paper-thin walls. I couldn't wait to get home, even though New England winters were not much better.

The last days of shows were always half days, and my flight from O'Hare to Logan was surprisingly on time. Geri was driving in with friends, and the plan was to have warm Chinese food in downtown Boston's Chinatown at 6 p.m.

Per usual, the indoor airport parking was not available, so I had parked on the roof. Upon arrival, the windows on my vehicle were frozen solid. I turned on the A/C to accelerate defrosting, but I froze my ass off because I was wearing a business suit and top coat. Forty-five minutes later, I departed for my last hurdle, the notorious Callahan Tunnel. It was just a few minutes' journey to downtown, but as every Bostonian knows, the tunnel traffic, prior to the opening of the Ted Williams Tunnel, could be cruel during rush hour.

This night was no exception. When my car suddenly stalled, the hope of arriving at the restaurant on time was gone for good. Every driver in the tunnel gave me the Callahan Finger, accompanied by beeping and loud cursing. I was in the tunnel for close to an hour.

I finally arrived at the restaurant as it was about to close, and Geri and our guests were nowhere in sight. Cell phones weren't invented until 1973, so there was no easy way to communicate.

I have purposely detailed this trivial event as it was the breaking point for me and I began to plan our escape from New England to LA.

COMBAT PAY

I thought I had the perfect job. My best friend was my boss, and I was young, driven, and on the fast track to being the first non-family VP at the company. My personal goal was to earn my VP stripes by age thirty.

I had a big advertising budget, and never really realized that with that big budget, you have a plethora of so-called friends but you also got a lot of nice perks. For example, I attended the first two Super Bowls in LA thanks to my agency, and Walter Murphy, our PR guy, arranged for us to have a forty-foot Hatteras yacht, complete with a captain, at our disposal during our personal vacation in Miami Beach. The problem with this was Geri immediately felt seasick when she boarded the boat and we never left the dock.

I also got Broadway tickets and box seats to watch the Red Sox at Fenway Park, even though I was a die-hard Yankees fan and hated to see Elston Howard, a former Yankee, behind the plate. My boss, Stephen Hassenfeld also loaned me the $2,500 I needed to put the downpayment on our first house.

Stephen also did a lot of little things that never went unnoticed. To get ready for the NYC Toy Show, the Peretz family was put up for three months at the luxurious Beekman Towers, just across the street from the UN Plaza. We had first class travel, a fancy company car, and a gasoline credit card.

Geri was invited on company trips, and I was invited to Hassenfeld family dinners so that I would feel like part of the family. I also received a generous yearly bonus. In addition, Stephen personally loaned me money towards a down payment on our house in Sharon, Massachusetts.

I recall bragging to friends and family that I went to London "not to ride a pony" for a single business lunch. We were pitching US distribution rights for Corgi die-cast vehicles. We had no downtime for socializing, and I worked on the plane with Stephen both ways.

Once, we needed to host a National Sales Meeting, and we couldn't find a date when our territorial sales representatives were available. So, we devised a solution. We held regional meetings at airports, beginning in the early morning, following time zone changes. The first stop was Boston, and we would finish in San Francisco. My best recollection of intermediate stops included New York, Memphis, Atlanta, Chicago, Dallas, and Los Angeles.

I was, however, paying a big price for my fame and fortune. My bags were always packed, I was always waiting for an emergency phone call, and there were frequent surprise dinner meetings. I even got called out for wearing shorts at a Saturday summer business meeting.

My average work week was seventy hours, and each week was filled with ups and downs and deadlines galore. The most challenging aspect of all though was that Stephen and his father often didn't see eye-to-eye. This resulted in two advertising budgets—one small one for Stephen's dad and the other, much larger one for Stephen.

My other big challenge was keeping up with Stephen. He had no other interests and worked all the time, whereas I had a household budget, a wife, a new baby, and a puppy.

It also didn't help that Stephen didn't have a sense of humor. This was illustrated rather horribly on what should have been a glorious day. The occasion was the introduction of the game Pie Face, the brainchild of our Chicago PR person, Aaron Cushman (who became a friendly tennis competitor of mine).

We rented an empty garage and invited the press to watch classic pie throwing footage, including Laurel and Hardy, and the Three Stooges. We had paddy wagons filled with pies for throwing, not eating.

I made my way to the garage, where there were actors dressed as keystone cops who began throwing pies around. Press cameras were rolling, and everyone got into the act except Stephen, who viewed the mayhem from a safe distance.

Jack Marks, my advertising manager, located Stephen and I couldn't stop him—he hit Stephen in the face with a pie. His actions were just too dumb to defend and I had to immediately fire him.

For those who follow the toy industry, Pie Face was a failure because players had to wear goggles to keep the pretend pie cream out of their eyes.

One day, I was having a drink at the Holiday Inn on Newport Avenue, near our factory, with Mike Detels, our advertising agency account executive who was excellent at his job. He knew how to put out fires. After he'd had a bit too much of the bubbly stuff, he gave me friendly advice that I took to heart. Mike said the only reason I had such an important position was because no one else would put up with the sh*t I put up with. He said I deserved combat pay, and he wasn't talking about GI Joe™.

All the dominoes leading to me leaving were falling into place by this time. Once I became a VP at age thirty, I lost some of my motivation. My right eye began twitching and the stress started to get to me. So, I went for a job interview for the position of President of Aurora. I had dinner with the owner, Chuck Dicker, in a distant spot. Somehow, though, word got back to Stephen and I passed on the job.

I finally exited Hasbro for a permanent position with the Kroffts in the Fall of 1969. I arrived at LAX the moment the Amazing Mets won the World Series.

I never spoke to Stephen again, although I did write a letter asking to come back and visit, but it went unanswered. Stephen ended up dying of AIDS at age forty-seven. I was in the Orient on business when he passed. If I had been state side, I would have attended the funeral and cried like a baby.

HR Pufnstuf Fun Fact:
The basic design and characters of
McDonald's "McDonaldland" commercials
were blatantly plagiarized from
H.R. Pufnstuf in 1971 after the Krofts
refused to license the Pufnstuf characters for
a McDonald's ad campaign.
The Kroffts sued in 1973,
and won in 1977.

X-RATED TALENT TURNS OUT G-RATED PRODUCT

As a result of GI Joe, Hasbro became a meaningful television advertiser. Previously, the budget was devoted entirely to SPOT television, market-by-market, but because of pressure from the national retail chains, the decision was made to devote part of the budget to the network. I was given a million dollars to spend on Saturday morning kid's television and it was divided between ABC, CBS, and NBC. A million dollars was a big deal for Hasbro, but in network parlance, it was a drop in the bucket, though new advertisers were highly sought after.

My initial meetings with the networks went as anticipated. We would be accepted as an advertiser—it was nothing to write home about. I pressed for a better outcome, and NBC advised there were a couple of crazy Greeks who were puppeteers and had a show concept titled *Lutherland*. Instead of Hanna-Barbera styled animation, there were costumed characters. With a show name change to *H.R. Pufnstuf*, Hasbro became the sole corporate sponsor, and the program became a huge hit.

Concurrently, I had burned out at Hasbro and made the move from Boston to Los Angeles to become the EVP of Sid and Marty Krofft Productions. From the distance of 2,500 miles away, Krofft's *World's Show Business Factory* seemed destined to become the next Disney.

Marty Krofft displaying some of the marionettes of Les Poupées de Paris *backstage at the 1962 Seattle World's Fair.*

REAMER, SKEEMER, AND DREAMER

When I arrived in North Hollywood, I learned there were not two but three Krofft brothers; the oldest, Harry, ran the back room and was never seen, so I nicknamed him the Reamer. Marty was the brains behind the operation and had the savvy of a used-car salesman, so I nicknamed him the Schemer. Sid was the undisciplined creative star who never saw a budget he couldn't exceed, so he, of course, was the Dreamer.

In summary, this business was run by X-rated people turning out G-rated products. Prior to children's television, they created *Les Poupées de Paris,* a risqué adult-oriented puppet show that played to nine million. I was so square and G-rated that I was completely out of my element. I didn't even realize that when the name of the show was changed to *H.R. Pufnstuf* it was referring to a drug connotation, i.e. smoking weed.

I tried following Marty, but never could catch up. He was on the fast track with Trudy, his assistant, following closely behind. I was instead writing position papers and handling routine marketing. I was also the contact person with Capitol Records, who had the rights to the *H.R. Pufnstuf* movie soundtrack.

Marty's wife, Christa, was a German beauty who in 1962 was named *Playmate* Centerfold of the Year. One day, Marty called me in to his office to meet celebrated photographer Mario Casilli, who had fifty-seven Playmate pictorials to his credit. Mario proudly showed me the pictures from Christa's shoot—Playboy was doing an anniversary edition. It was the first and last time I ever saw Marty's wife nude.

Billy Barty

LITTLE PEOPLE
END DAUGHTER'S CHILDHOOD

L ive puppets, or costume characters, comprised most of the cast for *H.R. Pufnstuf.* The talented little people behind these costumes included famous three-foot-nine actor Billy Barty, who was also an activist for people with dwarfism. In 1957, he founded Little People of America (LPA). Through the tireless efforts of Barty, Marty Krofft, and attorney Gary Concoff, the actor's union gave permission to have individual actors play multiple costume characters. Without this union concession, *Pufnstuf* would never have been made.

One of my favorite little people was a three-foot-nine guy with jet black hair and Hollywood good looks. He would get into a black Cadillac with long fins and cruise the Sunset Strip looking for "ladies of the night." He had a raised front seat and appeared normal height when driving, but when he opened the door and got out, the reaction of the ladies was not to be believed.

One day Lauren, my five-year old daughter, showed up on set at Paramount Studios to see her favorite TV show's characters in real life. She came on the set with Geri.

Upon their arrival, the production was dark, as the talent was on a lunch break. The characters' costumes were lined-up on the wall: heads, bodies, and feet. Lauren went over to Shirley Pufnstuf, touched her head, and asked, "What happened to the rest of you?" Her childhood had come to abrupt end.

Mama Cass

WHO DO I HAVE TO F♥-K TO GET OUT OF HERE?

The Krofft's crew were riding high. The new *Pufnstuf* movie featured a couple of cast additions: comedian Martha Raye and Mama Cass, formerly of the Mama and Papas. Cass sang the lead song, "Different," without rehearsing and had a perfect first take.

There was also the *Lidsville* TV show with costume characters living in hats. It starred one of my favorite comedians, Charles Nelson Reilly, who was always complaining about how long it took to put on his make-up. And also the *Bugaloos*, featuring a group of four teenagers selected from a heavily promoted talent call in London, home of Jack Wilde, the *H.R. Pufnstuf* star.

Understandably, the emphasis turned to creating new dark amusement park rides. A dark ride or ghost train in an indoor amusement park attraction is a ride in which passengers board guided vehicles that travel through specialty lit scenes. Such rides, produced by the Kroffts, were in Six Flag Amusement Parks in Atlanta and Dallas.

There was also the "The San Francisco Experience" on Fisherman's Wharf. They were also heavily involved in "The World of Sid & Marty Krofft" at Atlanta's Omni Center, which went out of existence in the 1970s in the biggest bust in theme park history.

There were also occasional high-profile assignments, like building a life size water bottle replica, designed by pop artist and sculptor Claes Oldenburg.

I clearly had to find something to do. I knew Kroffts' would never be the next Disney, and I realized, in retrospect, that my hiring was little more than a thank you for getting them on the air.

So, I decided to branch out into corporate America, using direct support from the talented crew that Sid had recruited and trained. I put together a dark ride spaceship with a graphics proposal and accompanying numbers for the H.F. Ahmanson Foundation. Ahmanson was one of the biggest holding companies in California, and their flagship was Home Savings and Loan.

I arranged for a high-level meeting of board members and senior executives, and Marty, who had never been part of the project, reluctantly agreed to show up—he would be out of his element, though. I was beginning my presentation, sitting at one end of the table with Marty at the other, when I received a folded note from Marty. The note read, "Who do I have to f♥-k to get out of here?"

Clearly, my days were numbered with the *Pufnstuf* gang, but I was in LA and it was still "The Golden Age." Shortly before departing, I arranged for a top tier licensing executive from New Jersey, Marty Appelto, to stop by on the chance that a big deal might be possible.

The Kroffts always overspent on projects and were looking for big bucks. After the tour of the Show Biz Factory, Marty Appel said something insightful: "They are super talented, but all I would be interested in is going through their garbage at the end of the day.

"When his marriage to Zsa Zsa was going south, Ryan disassembled Gabor's Rolls Royce and refused to put it back together again."

— Jerry Oppenheimer
from his book about Ryan, *Toy Monster: The Big, Bad World of Mattel.*

Jack Ryan standing in front of his "castle."

SECTION 9

PRETEND CASTLE

Jack Ryan (not the character in Tom Clancy's spy thrillers) was an ex-aerospace engineer turned toy designer who helped the Mattel founders, Elliot and Ruth Handler, move out of their garage. Surprisingly, Ruth handled the business side while Elliot was the creator. Ryan was at Mattel for twenty years as the VP of R&D. Their biggest early hits were Barbie™ in 1959, Chatty Cathy™ the following year, and Hot Wheels™ in 1968.

Jack was brilliant, as evidenced by his deal with Mattel, where he received a royalty that was reportedly 1.5 percent on every toy sold, regardless of whether he or anyone on his design team was involved in the invention. With Mattel growing every year, eventually to become the number-one toy company in the world, Jack quickly became a multi-millionaire.

In the early 1970s, with the Handlers no longer involved, Mattel changed Jack's deal to where items that lost money had their royalties subtracted from the total monies due. Big programs like the state-of-art Optigan Optical Organ failed and left Jack with no choice but to take legal action. During the legal proceedings, Mattel stopped all royalty payments. I was brought on-board to find new clients about this same time.

Jack's offices were anything but normal. He was residing in the old Warner Baxter estate on Nimes Road in Bel Air, which was built in 1933 by the famous actor of the 1910s. Jack added a bridge over a moat that went around the traditional Tudor home. He also installed a telephone system formerly used on a destroyer that chirped like a bird when the phone rang, and hired Janos Beny, a Hungarian Freedom Fighter and talented self-taught engineer as his castle keeper. There were also a vintage fire engine and a treehouse big enough to seat six with a dining room table and a chandelier above it on the grounds.

When we met there, lunch was prepared by a gourmet chef and served in the spacious dining room for all members of our group of between ten and twelve people.

Jack, who did a variety of drugs, loved women—especially the pretty ones— and they seemed to arrive at a moment's notice. The only eyesore at the castle was the paint on the office walls. Jack paid seven figures to acquire patents from the inventor of speckled paint, which came out of the can speckled, and he used it liberally. The problem was, the available color pallet was awful and the offices were extremely drab.

I had recently left an invention group, Innova, due to a lack of funds, before joining this new group. I made this move largely because I saw Jack Ryan residing in these plush surroundings and thought he was flush with money. I realized, upon actually joining the group and seeing no new major clients to replace Mattel, that this dream existence would soon be over.

JACK: NOT AN ENGINEER,
A SUPERSALESMAN/CON ARTIST

In theory, I was the salesman smart enough to step aside and watch the real professional, Jack Ryan, work. However, Jack, once a whiz kid engineer, was no longer a practicing engineer. When we went to see new clients, the rule was there were no engineers allowed in the room. Presentations were meant for top executives, from general management to marketing, sales, and finance. This meant Jack could answer soft questions from empty suits.

When prospective clients came to the castle, Jack conducted the tour. All design staff were present, but because of confidentiality, the ideas being worked on could not be shown. There were many closed doors that were marked "Top Secret, Employees Only" that went nowhere and were intended to impress. The grand finale lunch or dinner in the tree house was served by a waiter climbing the ladder. Polaroid™ pictures were also taken and handed out to everyone.

At Sears, Jack was talking to the sporting-goods buying group about Shimano brakes. He sat in the middle of the table, writing notes backwards and inside out. Even the most sophisticated and smartest clients couldn't resist wondering why Jack was writing in this unique and strange manner. Jack would tell them in a serious tone, "I'm inventing and I don't want anyone to see what it is."

We always traveled with a series of "B" sheet-sized product descriptions, leading with a folding guitar. The folding guitar always seemed simple and logical, and no one bothered with the details.

Louis Marx and Company, with its US headquarters located in Stamford, Connecticut, is now owned by British conglomerate Dunbee-Combee-Marx. The head of US operations was an ex-Mattel executive; need I say more. We were in their parking lot when Jack called from a heretofore unknown suitcase phone in his car. Invariably, when the client answered the call and Jack said, "We're in the parking lot calling from our phone." That little bit of impressive wealth seemed to be all it took to make the sale.

Traveling with Jack was always an experience. Later in the year, Jack and I were in London at the residency of Sir James Beechman COB, and we were invited for dinner. I remember during the cocktail hour I was bragging to a guest that we worked at a castle, when out came pictures of a real castle where she lived.

Proctor-Silex in Philadelphia was focusing on a new small appliance that made perfect French fries. While that was going on, the main focus for us became replacing Mattel with a major toy competitor. Ideal Toy took our bait, which involved in large part Jack's accomplishments and celebrity status.

ZSA ZSA CALLING

Jack's castle was frequently filled by Hollywood starlets. For example, Tyron Power's daughter, Taryn, was someone I talked to there regularly. I also vividly recall the day flamboyant financier Bernie Cornfeld sent a bus load of beauties to tease the designers.

All that changed when Jack married the Hungarian beauty Zsa Zsa Gabor. Zsa Zsa, who was Miss Budapest in 1933, was a star and socialite, as were her sisters, Eva and Magda. Jack, who was into having sex with stars, became Zsa Zsa's sixth husband in January 1975. It was a small wedding in Vegas, which I attended

The marriage lasted until august 1976, when Zsa Zsa filed for divorce. She would go on to marry six others. Before the divorce, Jack asked me to work with Zsa Zsa on her cosmetics line. I was not thrilled with this, because she was very difficult to work with and would never listen to anything I told her.

One time, Jack and I were in Paris on business, where Jack, of course, found time to fool around. This time it was with the star of *The Crazy Horse Saloon*. I was invited to join the two of them as part of a threesome, but I was happily married and cheating, even in Paris, was not on my bucket list.

When we were ready to leave Paris for LA, we arrived late at the new Charles de Gaulle airport. It was further away than Orly Airport, and we had left the luxury of the Charles V with not enough time to avoid Paris traffic.

Later, Zsa Zsa called Geri to tell her we were stuck in Paris and we would be home a day late. Geri said there was no mistaking she was talking to Zsa Zsa.

I must confess to leaving the Charles V with a monogrammed bathrobe. It seems I was not about cheating, but stealing was okay! As the great Boston Celtics announcer Chick Hearn would often say: "No harm, no foul!"

In a later Larry King interview, Zsa Zsa said, "I am a marvelous housekeeper; every time I leave a man, I keep his house."

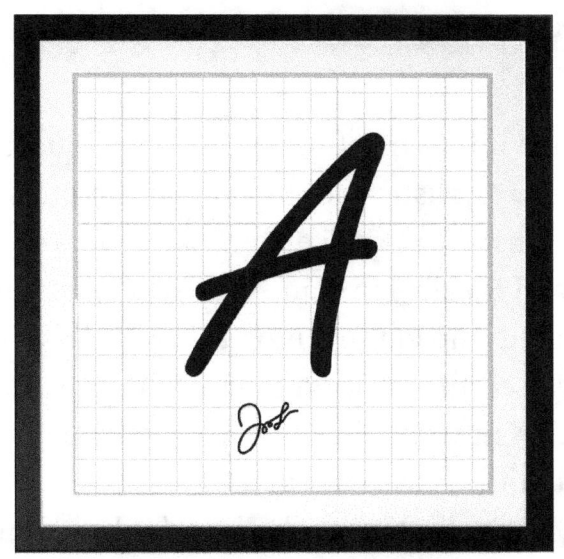

IDEAL DEAL IS DOOMED

When I closed the $3 million Ideal Toy deal, Jack Ryan, rather than giving me a bonus, gave me an "A" grade on my performance like I was still in school, then gave me a framed letter A he had drawn on a piece of graph paper and signed to mark the occasion. Ideal Toy was fresh off successes with Jaws, Rubik's Cube™, and Evil Knievel, and realized that the future of toys was in electronics, so moving to work with Ryan's group made sense.

Ideal included the number of team members required in their deal, as well as the number of visits per year from Bel Air, California, to Jamaica, New York, where the Queens headquarters was located. In exchange, Ryan received an advance against royalties of $3 million to be paid monthly, plus our commitment to not work for any other toy company.

During our initial meeting at Ideal headquarters, we presented a line of realistic-looking electronic guns. The VP of Dolls was against war toys, i.e. guns, and we were shot down. When I argued Ideal's Tin Can Alley was an air powered system from noted outside inventor Marvin Glass, CEO Lionel Weintraub closed the door on the idea by saying, "The difference between Tin Can Alley and your guns is ours sells and yours would not."

Back to Bel Air we went, with a laundry list of things to work on. We had exceptional engineering and design talent—almost all ex-Mattel people, including Dick May (who wore his lunch on his beard), J.D. Moore, Steve Bartok, Dave Weissman, Howard Dekan (stolen away from competitor Eddie Goldfarb), and the all-world model maker Bill Smedley, who was always seen trimming his mustache and checking out the ladies.

Jack only wanted engineers on the team, because according to him, all industrial designers did was put knobs on products. Large dolls were a big part of Ideal's line, and when it came to doll mechanisms, we were excellent. The question of who would handle the doll's appearance was every bit as important.

I had worked with Marilyn H., the best fashion designer on the planet. She was available, affordable, and interested. Marilyn presented her portfolio, which knocked everyone's socks off...except for Jack. True to form, he said, "Women are only for f**king."

Further complicating matters, there was Zsa Zsa, who took a healthy share of the Ideal advance dollars, as well as taking big chunks of Smedley's time to create and install a pair of electronic lions at the entrance to her mansion. Jack was also more interested in playing around than doing the work, and we were not living up to our deal requirements. Many of the staff members asked that I go directly to Ideal and tell them what was going on and offer to take over managing the deal.

One of my closest friends and my lawyer, Ron Scheinman, strongly advised against this approach, correctly saying, "Jack will sue your ass." I didn't do it. Predictably, we failed to perform and Ideal stopped paying advances. Jack closed the unit, and then raised the money to sue Ideal himself—a suit he would win.

Several years later, I left LA to work for Knickerbocker Toys, a Division of Time Warner. VP of Marketing there was headed by a good friend, Rod White, son of the founder. My family stayed behind while I lived in a Manhattan hotel for the time. Marketing in NYC was destined to move to New Jersey, so I looked for homes and decided upon one in Westfield.

My Realtor was Sylvia Cohen, and as she was showing me potential houses, I told her I was in the toy business. It turned out that I'd had bagels and lox in her home in Westfield when I was negotiating the Jack Ryan Ideal agreement with her husband, Sam Cohen, Ideal's legal head.

I recalled that Sam made the one-and-a-half hour commute each way through heavy traffic from Westfield to Jamaica, and I couldn't understand why. Long Island had wonderful towns. Sam told me, "I cannot leave where I live." I would eventually become a home owner in his town, and Sam's son would become my son's Little League baseball coach.

*"The crisis of today
is the joke of tomorrow."*

— H. G. Wells

THE SUN WILL COME UP TOMORROW

I moved to New Jersey in 1981 to become the Vice President of Marketing for Knickerbocker Toys, a division of Time Warner. The president of the company was a good friend (we later became partners), and he promised to take good care of me. The company was the largest stuffed toy manufacturer in the world, beginning with Raggedy Ann, and they specialized in licensed goods.

A result of the Time Warner acquisition was that company was expanding to new product areas. There seemed to be an enormous upside to this, except for one major hurdle—Stan H. was the EVP of Marketing and Sales. This meant he was my immediate boss, and going to Rod White, the son of the founder of Knickerbocker Toys, was out of bounds. Stan was shrewd and tricky and his ace in the hole was his close association with the number-one toy buyer in the country, TRU merchandising head Sy Ziv, who later promoted himself as a worldwide consultant.

I had an ace in the hole as well: Stan's significant other who worked for Stan Green. I had worked with this Stan while he was in charge of party goods with Hallmark Cards in Kansas City. I took full advantage of this.

NEVER RECEIVED THE NEEDED HEADS-UP

As I began my career at the Knickerbocker Manhattan office, I was told to fire Mike, the manager of packaging design. He worked at the factory in Middlesex, New Jersey. Mike got screwed when Knickerbocker was acquired by Time Warner, as he was a key player in building the business.

I had met Mike briefly and knew that while he was talented, he was also a bit of a loose cannon—he carried a knife in his sock.

So, I dictated the firing letter to a full-time temp and asked what she thought of the letter. She calmly said, "I'm Mike's mom. What do you think I think of it?"

I didn't know where to hide! This was embarrassing, to say the least.

I WAS HIRED TO RUN MARKETING, NOT TO BE A GARDENER

The factory got new offices in Middlesex, and they lacked almost all amenities, including windows. One day, the housekeeper came by to water the large potted Ficus plant near the entrance to my office. I was chastised for not watering it, but I replied that I honestly never noticed there was a plant there in the first place.

My secretary, Ms. Brady, who back then made all my phone calls and ran my personal errands, laughed hysterically. Later, she got her Irish up, accusing me of working too hard and having no life. Upon reflection, she was correct.

Members of the original Broadway cast for Annie:
Andrea McArdle as Annie, Reid Shelton as Daddy Warbucks,
and Sandy.

ORPHAN ANNIE
MADE ME A WINNER

*A*nnie, the musical opened on Broadway in 1977, and ran for six years, setting a record for the Alvin Theatre. The show was based on *Little Orphan Anny,* a comic strip by Harold Gray, which debuted in 1924. The Broadway show won seven Emmy Awards, including best musical. The Annie rag dolls made by Knickerbocker became unusually big sellers at the theater concession stands.

When Columbia Pictures announced there would be a movie version released in 1982, Knickerbocker outbid Mattel for the doll rights. We anticipated these rights to be worth

$100 million. I was charged with delivering a first-class introductory marketing campaign, which I did. It also won a few sales promotional awards along the way.

Just prior to our sales meeting at the toy show, with all the work done, Stan decided to fire me for no particular reason. We agreed on a timetable for the announcement of my replacement, agreeing it would not occur until after the show. This would be a good thing for my future employment within the toy industry.

I sat at a table comprised of my team and our advertising agency at the sales meeting. Stan was the MC for the meeting, and thanked everyone in sight except me, the guy who made it happen. Then to my shock, he brought my replacement up to the stage and with much fanfare introduced him. It didn't help my ego a bit that I knew him and knew he wasn't qualified to hold my jock strap!

My clueless staff sat there in disbelief. I decided that I had three choices: get up and leave, deliver a speech of defiance, or just sit there quietly thinking about how my long-term interests would best be served. I chose option three.

I later received a very generous financial settlement and left with my reputation intact. *Annie* the movie had a production budget of $35 million, and when the film opened on May 21, 1982, it was a box office disaster. It only made $59.1 million.

For Knickerbocker this meant Annie sales never materialized. Executive layoffs with no benefits soon followed, and later that year, Knickerbocker filed for bankruptcy.

MAY EVERY DAY BE A CIRCUS DAY

My parents took me to the circus every Spring when it made its way Madison Square Garden—it was a parental right-of-passage, and I did much the same for my kids. I found out the experience was very different as a parent. While the kids looked up in wonder, my attention was captured by the sanitation workers picking up the dung behind the elephants. It really was "The Greatest Show on Earth," as founder and showman, P.T. Barnum, said. He was also given credit for saying, "There's a sucker born every minute."

In the early 1980s, when I was active in the product development and licensing business, I had an idea to merchandise a circus make-up kit using the Ringling Bros. logo. I thought they could also sell the product at circus performances. I assumed the circus was headquartered in Florida but discovered they were actually just outside of Washington, D.C. in Upper Georgetown—a short flight from Newark to National Airport, a place that I would come to know quite well.

The Ringling headquarters was spectacular, and totally in keeping with the pizazz of the three-ring circus. When I got there though, the place was nearly empty. I arrived in the early morning, a make-up kit prototype in-hand, and soon learned that since performances were often at night, employees didn't start their day before 11 a.m. when the profit and loss statements for individual performances were miraculously distributed for the prior days' activities.

I was, however, greeted by a warm and friendly receptionist who greeted me with, "May every day be a circus day!" this was apparently a phrase widely used by all employees, including performers.

I was ushered in to meet with Chuck Smith, the CFO who had responsibility for Sales Floto, the division that handled all concession sales. Soon, the conversation switched to other matters: Chuck needed someone to temporarily manage Sales Floto. The current head, Frank Heltai, was on an extended personal leave. On January 29, 1982, Heltai was walking on 53rd Street in Midtown Manhattan next to comptroller Warren Levenberg, when Levenberg was suddenly and unbelievably decapitated by falling debris from a crane collapse above them. I quickly, as that was the Smith way of doing business, agreed to an arrangement to take the position. This required me to be at corporate weekly for the foreseeable future, but the pay was good.

NECESSARY JOB ATTIRE:
A DISGUISE:

I never met CEO Irvin Feld, or for that matter his son Kenneth. Instead, I took my marching orders solely from Chuck Smith, who advised me to stay low and out of sight. The only exception to the "hiding" rule was Joe Dugan, who became a trusted colleague. He, too, disappeared into the weeds (his weeds were in accounting).

Irvin, who was both respected and feared, was known to make frequent unannounced trips to view the performances, which would include small markets like Little Rock, where the mid-weekday matinee would draw crowds in the hundreds, not thousands. The circus would perform the same show regardless of attendance. To Irvin, attendance was irrelevant to the performance. Just to be certain, I wore a disguise to avoid the possibility of discovery.

Sales Floto was a cash business, and when the money was counted, if I was present, I would wear a bullet proof vest. The circus also hired its own muscle to make sure certain unauthorized concession goods were not being sold outside of the arena.

Irvin died September 6, 1984, and during his last act, he whispered something to Kenneth. There is a lot of debate as to what Irvin might have said, but the word on the street was Irvin, if he was still alive, would have allowed me to personally make the presentation because he would have known his business was in trouble and needed a change. Unfortunatly, Kenneth was heartless and was nothing like Irvin.

This hotel was made famous as result of the wiretapping of the Democrat Party's headquarters on June 17, 1972.

HIDING OUT IN THE INFAMOUS WATERGATE HOTEL

It became apparent that Chuck was making a play to take control of Ringling, although he never said so. Instead, I became an uncredited contributor to Chuck's dream by writing a business and marketing plan that described what was needed to reverse the years of significant attendance decline. The sales plan of Allen Bloom, VP of Sales & Marketing and Kenneth's right hand, was to put "asses in the seats" irrespective of what patrons paid for a ticket. There were many local partners who promoted the engagements, frequently giving away tickets for free.

All the profits were in concession sales from souvenir programs, lights, sno-cones, and cotton candy. Concession per caps went up every year. Sales Floto commission sellers, sometimes wanted felons, were the hungriest group of sellers I had ever encountered. They lived on the train with the merchandise, traveling from city to city. Some had relationships with the performers making that train a very private and potentially dangerous place.

I hid out at the Watergate hotel while I was writing the plan, and never left my room. Food was brought in, frequently pizza, sometimes delivered by Chuck. And there was, of course, room service. Any information I needed was sent by messenger. I had just two weeks to complete the assignment, meaning long days and little sleep. The result, I must admit, was a remarkable work titled "The Americanization of the Circus."

My plan advocated for the development of American talent that could be heavily promoted, instead of usual performers from legendary circus families, many from Eastern Europe. Kenneth was all about maintaining circus traditions at any cost, and this had caused the business to be in serious trouble. Smith knew it was his time to pounce.

When it was finished, I assumed I would be let out of jail to make the presentation, but that never happened. In the end, that was okay because Chuck gave me a ten thousand dollar bonus for two weeks of work, which was a substantial amount at the time. We shook hands, never to touch base again.

The circus folded its tents after 146 years on May 21, 2017. Kenneth and his sister Karen disagreed on just about everything, and a brutal court battle that would take years ensued. Interestingly, I recently read that Feld Entertainment is bringing the circus back in 2023, without animals.

CLOSE, BUT NO CIGAR, KID!

TOY KNOCKOUT!

SECTION 12

CLOSE BUT NO CIGARS

There are two kinds of people: those in the arena who play the game, and those in the stands who watch, often second guessing and armchair coaching, not realizing there is no second guess. (In one of my sports books, I made the observation that the number-one sport in America is the second guess.)

While it is much safer in the stands, it's much more exciting to be part of the action, even when you fail. As the Japanese saying goes, *"Nana Korobi ya oki,"* which translates to "Fall down seven times, get up eight." Having a sense of humor can make the difference in recovering from numerous failures —

the alternative would be to spend the rest of your life as a spectator, preferably in either a box seat or orchestra middle.

New ideas fail most of the time—believe it or not, about 90 percent of the time! I'm an expert on this subject. There is a fine line between passion, which is good, and falling in love with your creation, which is dangerous.

There are numerous reasons for failure: unrealistic expectations; concepts often look good on paper but don't translate dimensionally; always about reducing to practice or execution; creating a development calendar that often has a high hurdle (nothing in business happens without a deadline); a shortage of working capital; being pre-empted by competition; principals who don't get along or see the fork in the road differently; and then there are external factors, including new competition, luck, timing, etc.

The issue for me is that I was not focused. I always had too many balls/ideas in the air, but they were not pertinent. Most of these ideas were presented for third party licensing—the risk takers—not for my account.

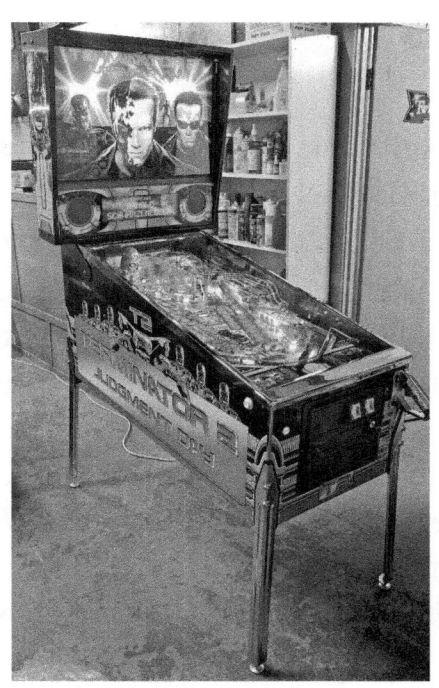

TOO MANY SALES IS A BAD THING

The *Portable Hand-Held Pinball machine*, one of my earliest inventions, was created to fill a major market void. A regular sized pinball machine measured 51" wide and 75.5 long and was not suitable for home use. Pinball first became popular during the depression as low-cost form of entertainment. The hand-held device I envisioned was 4" wide and 6 inches tall, with a thickness of 2 inches. This was an engineering challenge, as the feel and speed of the ball and flippers were critical to authentic pinball play

I found a mechanical engineer in the Valley who, after several tries, solved the problem. Then, I hired Elliot Rudell, a talented graphics designer and a born-again Christian, for the game board and packaging graphics. He showed up at our meeting holding a Bible.

As we negotiated his fees, Elliot wanted to be paid by the hour, while I insisted on a cost to complete the entire job. Elliot said it would take, I believe, seventy-three hours. When I asked him for the delivery date, he said tomorrow morning. We all laughed.

The first company we showed the game to was Parker Bros. They paid an advance and then passed. Atari (part of Time Warner) and Milton Bradley did the same thing—a rare occurrence, indeed. At least the advances covered the development costs.

A year later, a small start-up called Castle Toys introduced a hand-held game similar to mine. Interestingly, the company founder, Paul S., took my position when I departed from Hasbro.

I DIDN'T LIKE RAISINS ANYWAY

My next venture was in animated sports trading cards. Called Thumbshots, these cards were flip books with player stats on the back. The play pattern was identical to the flip books created by independent designer Hal Brandeis, so we formed a new business called Pocket Money Sports, and become the exclusive licensee.

Hal sourced and handled the printing and, most importantly, the binding. It was magical flipping through the book, watching Kareem Abdul Jabbar's sky hook from start to finish. Outside investors were so excited that we quickly raised $250,000 for a can't miss idea (as all of the ideas in "Almost Winners" start).

I negotiated licensing agreements with the NBA/NBAPA and, most importantly, the MLB/MLBPA. During the MLBPA meeting, I sat across the table from Marvin Miller, the man who started the unionization movement of professional athletes. We acquired the needed rights but the royalty rates were out of sight thanks to Marvin—if you wanted the jersey from the MLB and the players from MLBPA, you had no other option but to pay double royalties.

I sourced the images by retaining the services of a Los Angeles Dodgers photographer who traveled across the country to reach his quota of needed pictures. We had Rod Carew bunting, Pete "Charlie Hustle" Rose stealing second, and Steve Garvey swinging, among others—all in actual game situations.

We made a retail distribution deal with the president of Dell in NYC, knowing the action would be in premium sales, not retail. And we finalized a major promotion with Post Raisin Bran, and worked hard to develop a miniature book that could be packed in a cereal box at the required cost of less than $.03 per box. This was a major feat that Hal accomplished.

The numbers were huge but, unbelievably, there was a shortfall of the raisin crop at Sun Maid in California due to weather. That year there were not enough raisins to support a national promotional campaign. So, the campaign was canceled.

The licensing contact with MLB/MLBPA was one-year deal with expensive renewals, so our working capital ran out. The original investors passed on a second round of financing.

EVEN BARBARA EDEN
COULD NOT SAVE ME

I was introduced to Emmy award-winning television producer Danny Arnold of Four D Productions, who produced *Barney Miller, That Girl* and *Bewitched*. Barney Miller was one of my favorite sitcoms. It ran for eight seasons, from 1975 to 1982, and had 170 episodes. Today I watch reruns on cable. The cast of characters from the NYC 6th Avenue police department in Greenwich Village still holds up—funny is funny.

Danny was producing a new NBC show for Barbara Eden of *I Dream of Jeannie* fame. That show ran for five seasons, from 1965-1970, and had 139 episodes. Eden even has a star appears on the Hollywood Walk of Fame . The new series was to be about the toy business, and the pilot was about an adult little-person spy pretending to be a child at a research session for evaluating new toys.

I was hired as the toy consultant, which included a screen credit. The pilot was not well received, and the show was canceled. Many in the industry claimed the cancellation was the result of Arnold's frustration with the network, and that is indeed possible. He was known to have butted heads with television executives over content and schedules for years.

Mel Blanc and his son Noel.

CHILDREN'S BEDTIME RADIO: PUT THE STATION TO SLEEP

Isat in on many research sessions over the years with the Gene Reilley Research Group in which mothers expressed the importance and benefits of telling bedtime stories to children. The problem was, parents often didn't have the time to do this. I sensed a business opportunity for a product to fill this void. So we formed *Children's Bedtime Radio* with Joel Davis, a friend and a broadcast media expert. I would take care of the creative, and Joel would deal with the station lineup.

We retained the design services of Kathy Bleser, an ex-Mattel employee, to create the storyline. We had the first show produced by Noel Blanc who, with his father Mel Blanc, formed Blanc Communications Corporation. They largely produced public service announcements (PSAs).

Mel, who was a legend in the animation business, creating the voices for a range of characters, including Bugs Bunny ("What's up doc?"), Daffy Duck, and Porky Pig. The talented Noel, who also did voices, produced a sample show complete with original characters, voice-overs, a music soundtrack, and special effects. The format was a short segment, just enough to tell a bedtime story.

Joel went out to the stations to syndicate Bedtime Radio, but was unsuccessful. Stations were not happy with the idea that the radio was turned off after the child was put to bed.

Side note: Radio Disney, which started in 1996 and closed in 2021, featured music programming oriented specifically toward children, pre-teens and teenagers.

Billie Jean King and Bobby Riggs.

BILLIE JEAN KING LOVED DOLL BUT THOUGHT IT WAS UGLY

Billie Jean King was the biggest female tennis star in the game in the early 1970s. She enjoyed a number-one ranking and became a worldwide celebrity. In one of the most hyped events in sports history, "The Battle of the Sexes," which took place on September 20, 1973 at Houston's Astrodome, the twenty-nine year old defeated the hustler and gambler, fifty-five year old Bobby Riggs in three straight sets: 6-4, 6-3, 6-3 as ninety million worldwide viewers watched.

Because of her fame and popularity, she had become the spokesperson for Colgate Toothpaste. I received approval from Colgate to create a doll of King that they would use as a premium. I retained the services of Barbara Bleser, cousin of Kathy Bleser, the best soft doll designer in Los Angeles to create the doll.

She nailed King's appearance—the likeness was uncanny. Celebrity approval was necessary, and I thought we had a winner. We presented the doll to Billie Jean King, who was seated with husband Larry, at a court-side box at the 1974 US Open, held in Forest Hill, New York, at the Westside Tennis Club. (Side note: the 1974 US Open was the last year the tournament was played on grass.)

Billie Jean commented that the doll looked *exactly* like her, and I was just about to take a bow. Then she said. "This doll is ugly. It's got buck teeth, a flat chest, it's short and a little portly, and it's wearing glasses."

King, of course, was correct. In my attempt to get her approval—celebrity approval is not easily obtained—I lost sight of the fact that King was, indeed, unattractive. So, the doll was a no-go.

Looks be damned, King would win the finals, defeating adorable Australian Aborigine Wiradjuri Evonne Goolagong 3-6, 6-3, and 7-5.

I was a big tennis fan and a decent club player. I had an opportunity as a guest to play on the Westside grass courts and shower in their clubhouse afterwards. When I looked over, I saw Australian Fred Stolle, who reached number three in the world, also showering, and I remember thinking to myself, *We have the same equipment. Why are his strokes so much better?*

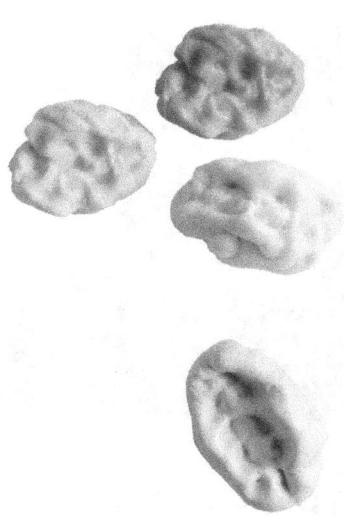

CIRCUS BUBBLE GUM BLEW-UP

Ringling Bros. Barnum and Bailey had a significant concession business, Sales Floto. Two novelty food items were among their best sellers: cotton candy and sno-cones. My idea was so obvious—circus bubble gum—that I was almost embarrassed to ask for a royalty payment.

I sourced the gum from an established supplier and utilized Ringling art for the gum wrapper. It received enthusiastic and immediate approval from my friend and head honcho, Chuck Smith. Legal reared its ugly head though, rejecting the product because three children choked from swallowing bubble gum the previous year. Any child's death that can be avoided should be avoided, so there was no circus gum. The quality of circus novelties would never get Consumer Products Safety Commission approval, and we were thankful they did not have jurisdiction over circus novelties.

JIMMY CARTER SHOULD HAVE STAYED A PEANUT FARMER

The Hamp Bag—a practical invention—had the appearance of a laundry bag with the gusset on its back, which give the bag the capacity of a hamper. It could be easily hung on the back of a bathroom door. I went to Taiwan several times to source this product.

The major concerns were finding a selection of vinyl bathroom fashion colors, and the construction of the contemporary triangle-shaped packaging that could stand up. When I arrived at the factory in the mid-seventies, a vendor was mixing colors with a paddle in a barrel, hoping to get the right shade of burgundy. This was a time-consuming process, and the result was often not the required perfect match.

To solve this problem, I brought The Pantone Matching System Plastic Standard Chips Collection on the next trip—I felt like Marco Polo.

Hamp bags were sold in the notions sections of major department stores, as well as to Linens and Things and Bed Bath and Beyond. The sales volume was not impressive at the start, but we were building as the product retailed.

A big break came when Jake Williams, an ex-Marine and the towel buyer for JCPenney, approached us. Penney owned the white goods business at that time, and their towel was the number-one selling towel in the country.

Penney started putting us in small catalogs, and over time we got into bigger and bigger books. Williams was going to be at the Penney regional office in Santa Ana, California, and he asked me to drive down from LA to meet with him because he had good news to share.

At this point we were doing low six figures, and he handed me an order for over a million dollars. The order consisted of special colors, pre-ticketing, and different case packaging. His big concern was whether we could deliver on a timely basis. Of course, I said yes, even though I knew the required delivery dates were ambitious. The drive back to LA was one of the best moments in my business career.

We secured working capital financing from one of the factors at 1440 Broadway in Manhattan, using the signed contract from JCPenney as collateral. Factors are secured creditors who advance money toward receivables and inventory, which banks don't tend to do. They also charge a much higher interest rates than traditional banks — 22 percent compared to the banks at 18%. (I believe these particular factors were referred to as the 40 thieves.) Payments from JCP went directly to them and the factors opened letters of credit, enabling the factory in Taiwan to be paid when the goods arrived at the docks.

Then the unthinkable happened. Thanks to President Carter and the 1979 Iran hostage crisis, the US economy tanked.

Williams sent me a telegram saying, "If you don't own it, you don't own it." Translation: special goods for JCPenney are in our warehouse, not theirs. Signed contracts as previously written did not have a takeout date, and while the order would be honored, we would not be paid.

The business folded.

AL ANDERSON WAS GIFTED,
BUT IDEAL GOT COLD FEET

It was apparent that in Los Angeles in the seventies, skate-boarding—like The Beach Boys—was about to sweep the country. The turning point was the 1975 Del Mar National Championships, where 500 skateboarders participated.

We needed a talented individual to create a toy response to the fad, and the designer of choice was Al Anderson, who resided in Topanga Canyon, just up the Ventura Freeway from my residence in Encino.

Al, who made most of his living making models for Mattel, was a talented designer but he was hampered by personal issues. We had worked on two small projects previously and made money: the Showdown Sam ping-pong gun action game (licensed to Miner Industries); a chocolate concentration game, where the pieces looked like those in a box of Whitman chocolates; and Pressman Toys.

I bent over backwards to accommodate his concerns, like having the licensee send 50 percent of the royalties directly to him. I stopped by weekly to say hello and hold his hand. On this particular day, Al agreed to start creating a skateboard toy.

In a matter of days—not weeks or months—Al, as he most often did, hit a home run. The product was called Sidewalk Surfers. It was made up of six bendable/poseable figures in a 6-inch high wire form armature. The skateboarders looked the part, and once posed, they could perform tricks.

I knew I had a huge item with no product issues (like safety), and I was off to Ideal Toys in Jamaica, Queens, to see Julie Cooper, the head of R&D. The immediate smile on Julie's face said it all. Ideal executives were ushered into the conference room, where I was hugged and, believe it or not, kissed. Everyone in the room believed this would be their number-one product in the Toy Fair line.

I left later that day with a signed agreement and an advance check, which was uncommon in the industry. I got home, went immediately to Al, gave him his check and a copy of agreement he needed to sign. Al was so pleased that he started on one of my pet projects: miniature games based on Guinness World Records. It involved swallowing a goldfish and how many individuals could be stuffed into a telephone booth.

I went to the Ideal Toy Showroom at the Toy Building in NYC, and Julie took me around. To my astonishment, Sidewalk Surfers was not displayed. Julie said two weeks after my presentation, another inventor, Eddie Goldfarb and Assoc., came in with a similar item. Even though it was not as well executed, Ideal got cold feet. They were worried that skateboard toys would be everywhere and they became paranoid. Not a single skateboard toy was introduced that year, and the opportunity was forever lost.

I haven't spoken with Al since the seventies, but his etching of me holding a Peretz monogrammed wooden tennis racket is one of my favorite possessions.

FIVE MILLION IN SALES
NOT ENOUGH FOR HALLMARK

Dimensional Greetings was an innovative product line of small delicate soft sculptures. Instead of sending a greeting card, you could send a soft dimensional toy. These included: a bottle of wine, peace doves, a birthday cake, a graduation cap, a bouquet of roses, etc. The packaging was unique as well. The item came in a see-through box that doubled as a mailer.

Husband and wife team Jonathan and Lynn Shook did all the flat and dimensional design work. The execution was every bit as good as the idea—a rarity. I remember thinking, *If I was smart, I'd drop everything else and form a new business.* Turns out I wasn't that smart.

Instead, I set my sites on getting into Hallmark Cards, which had a reputation of not looking at items from the outside. They owned the gift business with 40,000 stores carrying their card line, and they had an ability to diversify well beyond cards. Then, in 1973, Keepsake Ornaments were launched. Today, the number of individual ornaments is in excess of 8,000. I did manage to wiggle my way to a command performance in front of a group of senior executives though.

After the meeting ended, I was ushered into a room where a complete line of Hallmark classic games like checkers and chess, were on display. I was asked to determine the marketability of the line, and I did so. I said the games were not commercial. I was being tested and passed with flying colors, as the test market results for these were disappointing.

Next on their agenda was a decision of *Dimensional Greetings*. They were impressed by the thinking and the designs, but candidly said, "We don't see the line doing more than five million dollars in sales annually. It's hardly worth the effort of going to the Orient to single source these soft toys."

But they were not through with me. They offered me a generous consulting assignment fee, where I would become the juvenile expert for party goods. Hallmark Cards knew nothing about the children's market and were stuck in the past.

So, I decided to help them revamp the pricing for their party goods, which were priced way too high. The first thing I decided to change was to remove the nut cup (it was meant to hold individual servings of nuts). Apparently, this item was a Hallmark tradition and my idea was booed.

The work was stimulating and the people were first rate. The assignment was challenging. Kids were not giving or sending greeting cards—the enemy was the telephone. My chore, find out what, if anything, Hallmark could do about it.

In the meantime, I also believed I could take *Dimensional Greetings* to other companies, and so I did. Gibson Greetings in Cincinnati, Ohio, was a top-five greeting card industry supplier, and they were next on my target list. Their reaction to my presentation was the best I have ever received—I got a standing ovation from all those present.

Unfortunately, they had no capability or interest in manufacturing soft toys in the Orient—it was outside their product scope. There was a deal to be made, but there was a catch: I would have to move to Cincinnati. They offered a royalty carrot and moving costs as my incentive.

Vampirella was popular among cosplayers at conventions. Two of the earliest, flanking creator Forest J. Ackerman, were Angelique Trouvere on the left and Charlene Brinkman on the right.

STAR WARS DEVOURS THE ROOK

Western Superhero time traveler, *The Rook* seemed on its way to success. The self- taught engineer, Janos Beny, formerly of the Jack Ryan Group, built the prototype. It was a new type of action figure featuring unique new play pattern: a visible belt timer on the figure, forcing the action to be completed before the figure fell over.

To promote *The Rook*, I made a deal with Jim Warren, who founded Warren Publications in 1957. Warren specialized in hero-fantasy science-fiction in magazine format, bypassing the restrictive comic book code. I chose Warren as a result of the popularity of Vampirella, a fictional vampire super heroine introduced in 1969 . (I also developed a fondness for Jim Warren because he flew secret missions for the Israeli Air Force.)

Four *Rook* comics were completed, and on the road I went, showing the comics and the prototype figure to everyone I met. Interest was high among several potential licensees. Then along came Star War figures in 1978, which totally devoured the action figure market. Reportedly, between 1978 and 1985, 300 million Star Wars figures were sold.

UNITED NATIONS GIFT SHOP MANAGER: PEACE DOES NOT SELL

Mary Engelbreit, a gifted illustrator of greeting cards, books, and calendars, began her career in the second grade. Upon receiving a pair of eyeglasses from her Mother, the world around her opened up. You can see this in many of her illustrations. The artist, based in Clayton, Missouri, often wears signature glasses and a wide hat.

After visiting Mary at her first company store, Starshine (which I was a principal of), we entered into an exclusive licensing agreement for ceramics and stuffed toys. Mary was a joy to work with. She even agreed to attend the Annual Collectibles Show in South Bend, Indiana, and assisted in our packaging designs (although demanding final product approval given on a timely basis).

Her illustrations were detailed and whimsical. My favorite ceramic was one on an arm chair with the words "Life is a Chair of Bowlies." I also liked an illustration she did of a majestic lion and dressed in a velvet robe wearing a crown and holding a lamb in his arms. Her dimensional execution was superb.

My partner, Rod White, had built Knickerbocker Toys into the largest stuffed toy company in the world, and it was time to visit retailers. My introductory plan was to start at the UN Gift Shop and to heavily publicize the arrival of the lion and lamb.

I was warmly greeted by the manager there. I lovingly showed lion and lamb item, only to receive the most disappointing reaction to a new product in my lifetime. The manager said, "Not interested. Peace does not sell."

City Sign Dolls: Texas, LA, New England

PLACES OF INTEREST ARE NOT OF INTEREST TO LITTLE GIRLS

Back in the early twentieth century, collecting dolls of the world was commonplace for little girls. My concept, City Sign Dolls, was to replace the cities of the world with major cities in the United States. American Girl proved doll collecting every bit as important as traditional doll play.

Further, City Sign Doll had great components: soft construction that could meet small-parts safety standards, a street sign cleverly doubling as a doll stand, and a four-color mini travel guide describing points of interest for little girls. We also had award-winning packaging created by Smith Design of Glen Rock, New Jersey.

The challenge was to find a doll designer who could clothe the individual dolls in traditional but contemporary fashion. We wanted you to be able to recognize the dolls' geographic location by their appearance. There were twelve dolls in the original collection, with cities including Boston, New York City, Atlanta, New Orleans, Dallas, Chicago, Denver, San Francisco, and Los Angeles.

I selected Stephanie J., who I had previously worked with on Sweet Faith, the top selling religious doll of all time. Prior to Sweet Faith, religious dolls were largely unattractive, but in the hands of Stephanie, we proved that a beautiful religious-themed doll mass market was suitable and Sweet Faith became a hit.

City Sign dolls were beautifully executed by Stephanie, but DSI (the licensee, the same company that previously marketed Sweet Faith) was in the process of being sold, so necessary promotional dollars were not available. Subsequent market research proved mothers loved the concept, but their daughters were far less enthusiastic. Places of interest, travel, and geography are not what the girls really cared about.

PLEAD GUILTY TO PROMOTING CASUAL SEX WITHOUT KNOWING

Hook-ups were a line of trendy, fashion-edge soft dolls for young teenage girls, designed by Marilyn H. I worked with Marilyn for years, and we became good friends.

She was born in Toronto and married a well-known TV personality, who then left her for TV star Suzanne Somers—a younger version of herself. Marilyn was cute and petite and always dressed in jean shorts and spiked heels. She was hip to current fashion trends, and her newest doll line, Hook-ups, seemed destined for success.

The dolls were called Hook-ups because each of the twelve dolls in the line came with a plastic hook that attached to a backpack—something nearly every girl took to school. Walmart and KayBee Toys both added the line to their planograms, and the industry buzz was awesome.

All that changed seemingly overnight when Walmart, responding to a single parental call, dropped the line. We had no idea that the phrase "hook-ups" had a secondary meaning that the retailer found offensive.

What we soon found out was, although there are various definitions, researchers generally agree that hooking-up involves "casual sexual-behavior, ranging from kissing to intercourse with a partner, in which there is no current relationship commitment and no expected future relationship commitment."

and his friends

McDONALD'S DEALS A FATAL BLOW TO KING GOODMUNCH

K ing Goodmunch was created as an animated television short to promote good nutrition to children. The push for nutrition labeling on packaging began in 1972. I retained the services of a graphics designer from Little Silver, New Jersey, and a nutrition educator, who belonged to a nonprofit organization founded in 1968, renamed the Society of Nutrition Education and Behavior (SNEB).

We created a family of characters under the King Goodmunch umbrella, including bad guys named the Nasty Habits. Accompanying the art was a pioneering list of nutritional guidelines for children that was prepared by a nutritionist. I was to be a presenter at the annual meeting.

Goodmunch was well received by the membership in attendance, but most of the meeting was confined to a heated debate regarding SNEB guidelines and whether they should they be aimed at the perfect child or the good child? A good child is a child who cheats a little bit—say having French fries couple times a week. It was a typical non-profit group of well-meaning do-gooders who debated but accomplished little.

I was looking for an endorsement from SNEB before going to Nabisco and Nickelodeon. The endorsement never materialized. The inside scoop was that McDonald's, who through their Happy Meals merchandises unhealthy foods, was SNEB's largest donor. One of my Nasty Habit characters was a French-fried potato, so I'm sure that didn't go over well.

This reminds me of Virginia Slims, the Philip Morris cigarette brand, becoming the sponsor for women's professional tennis. Members were apparently willing to promote smoking to get the circuit launched.

Ralph Edwards executive producer of The People's Court. *He also produced and hosted* This Is Your Life, *which ran on NBC-TV for 37 years.*

PEOPLE'S COURT JUDGE FORGOT HE WAS NOT IN HIS COURTROOM

Brown and Bigelow, located in Saint Paul, Minnesota, started in 1856 and is known for manufacturing custom calendars. They also had a small division, Hoyle, which was the second largest producer of playing cards. Bicycle was the industry leader in that category, and they dominated the Las Vegas gambling business because their cards had a good snap in its cards. Hoyle's business was never able to penetrate that market.

Hoyle did have one asset—its name, which derived from the British writer Edmond Hoyle of *According to Hoyle* fame. I was retained to turn Hoyle into a game company. Our first product was a home run Pocket Trivia—or Trivia for a Buck.

Pocket Trivia was a clever, inexpensive knockoff of Trivial Pursuit, introduced in 1981. This version could be played without the expensive playing board.

To build Hoyle to a full-line game brand, under the effective leadership of Rick Farrell, I visited Los Angeles to acquire the board game rights for the popular television court drama *The People's Court*. I shook hands with Ralph Edwards, the executive producer known worldwide for hosting *This Is Your Life*. He was charming and entertaining, and his only complaint was that he had delivered too many eulogies.

The next part of the program was game creation, and I successfully reached out to Paul Gruen of West Newbury, Massachusetts—a noted board game inventor. I also contacted his Disney-trained cartoonist pal Peter Panas, to create the first Hoyle character. There was no existing art on Edmond Hoyle in the archives.

To kickoff the game at Toy Fair in NYC, the Hoyle sales force brought in the celebrity Judge Joseph Wapner—the star of *The People's Court*—for fifteen minutes (the sellers were available for an hour, and we had a full line of merchandise to present). The judge surprisingly arrived in his robes, adored the adulation, and took questions. We couldn't get him off his podium. When he finished one hour later, he received a standing ovation and had completely ruined our meeting.

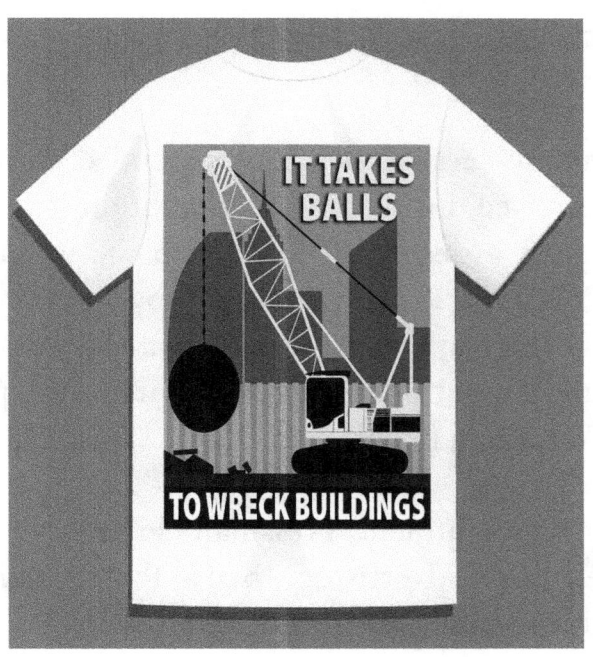

DEMOLITION TOY IDEA
GETS HIT BY WRECKING BALL

I was teaching an introductory sales course at the NYU School of Commerce, and my students were not watching or listening on this particular day because a building was being demolished directly across the street from the classroom. Their fascination with this was not surprising, and it became the genesis for an action game I presented to Pressman Toys (who I had a healthy working relationship with).

I visited several times with the president of The Cleveland Wrecking Company. This business was the industry leader in this very profitable but risky enterprise. I found out that all of the profits for each of their jobs depended on the value of materials removed during precise demolition.

I had made a decorated wooden block-building proto-type and a plastic crane to use for the toy. They were built to demonstrate the play pattern. I anticipated Pressman would tool the building out of plastic. As a part of the promotion, Cleveland Wrecking furnished a T-shirt slogan, "It takes balls to wreck buildings."

To my disappointment, Pressman elected not to tool the game for television advertising. Then at the toy fair, the prod-uct was hidden in the back showroom.

NECESSITY IS NOT
THE MOTHER OF INVENTION

I became a member of Health Quest physical fitness club in Flemington, New Jersey, located within a spitting distance of my new office. It was a log cabin overlooking a brook. The facility included NBA-quality basketball courts, a swimming pool, and an outdoor lighted baseball stadium.

On the first day, I went into the spacious men's locker room and noticed all combination locks had black faces. This made finding your locker an adventure. It seemed very confusing, especially since, unknowingly, I was in the beginning stages of becoming visually impaired from orbital cancer.

I reached out to Derek Gable, an ex-Mattel employee and "Brit who loved America." He was a first class mechanical engineer, smartly residing in Palos Verdes, California. I knew Derek from the toy business where he had been, among other things, the head designer behind Mattel's Masters of the Universe. One of his most profitable inventions was the real estate lock box.

In a matter of weeks, Derek solved the lock problem by inventing a small clear plastic container with a lid that fit directly over the lock. The container opened and a four-color image could be inserted into it. Images ranged from licensed to custom art. I started future buyer presentations using a picture of myself.

The registered descriptive name for this product was PictureLocks. Armed with prototypes, I went to the Hardware Show in Las Vegas. This was the first time I was at this venue. I discovered no direct competition, and the salespeople were genuinely excited by the product.

I followed this with a sourcing trip to Hong Kong. I needed to find a manufacturer who could duplicate the industry's best-selling combination lock: a padlock from Master Lock. Their lock was the industry leader, with more than an 80 percent market share.

The marketing thrust entered into exclusive licensing agreements with major professional sport leagues (with the exception of the NFL, who were not in the business of single item licensing). The major packaging innovation was to incorporate 30 major league baseball teams on one pegged card, enabling a mass market boxed retailer like Target to devote just one 4" x 6" peg to the product, while featuring every baseball team. This would avoid the problem of inventory, balancing the kiss of death.

I visited Walmart in inconvenient Bentonville, Arkansas, many times, and received a commitment for 250,000 Picture-

Locks units. I had been warned repeatedly by many others of the danger of doing business with Walmart. With over 3,000 stores, they would become the big gorilla. The result would be all your eggs in one basket.

Not surprisingly I got screwed, as the hardware buyer I had cultivated for close to eighteen months was transferred, and his replacement canceled the order. He viewed the item as a back-to-school product, not a line hardware product.

He turned out to be right, as the other big chains, Target, American Hardware, and Kmart felt much the same way. Back-to-school is a seasonal business, typically merchandised in outposts, not in the hardware department. We were unable to modify the merchandising plan on the fly and missed the season.

"If a cluttered desk
is a sign of a cluttered mind,
of what, then, is an empty desk a sign?"
—Thomas Edison,

SECTION 13

CLUTTERED DESK, CLUTTERED MIND?

French philosopher Voltaire's novella *Candide* made the point that gardening is "an extraordinary way to keep busy." This philosophy must have affected me deeply because I had a strong work ethic at age eighteen, when I started making my mark in the world. Another reason I was driven is that when my dad died unexpectedly while I was a sophomore at the University of Vermont, I had to come home to NYC to assist my mother in recovering from a nervous breakdown. Rather than grieving—it hurt too deep—I decided instead to grow up.

I did so by getting a full-ride scholarship from New York University and by doing part-time and summer work. Much later in life, I turned to yoga because learning how to relax is a wonderful tonic to being busy, busy, busy.

BLOOMINGDALES
WHITE FLOWER ABUSE

I was selected by Martha Scudder to join the Bloomingdales Summer Executive Training Program in 1960, when the store was widely considered the best department store in the world. Prior to Scudder, the only way to become a head department buyer was when the buyer passed away.

Assignments included Young World, where children's goods were separated not by product categories (the normal practice) but by recognized designers and high-priced fabrics sold by the yard. I didn't like the action, because to me, the real challenge was getting the merchandise from the factory to the retail floor.

Physical inventories were taken every January, and buyers' evaluations were made and bonus determined by the value of the inventory. A big problem was inventory shrinkage. It was an exciting moment when I observed the elimination of night floor merchandise theft—the watchmen who needed watching were replaced by German Shepherds.

There were many reasons why the store was at its peak:. The first was location. It was on the prestigious 59th Street East side location, made possible by the May 12, 1955, phasing out of the IRT Third Avenue elevated line. Then there was a first floor cosmetics department, highlighted by make-up artists at every counter, and a Third Avenue Men's Department at the store entrance. There were also free monogrammed shopping bags, which spread the store's logo all over the city. and finally, an integral part of the Bloomingdales philosophy was to take back any merchandise a customer wanted to return, regardless of condition—with no questions asked.

In the fall of 1960, after I finished school, I worked nights and weekends as a Divisional Superintendent (DS). This simply meaning that I wore a white flower, making me the target for customer returns. I was constantly abused, mostly when women's shoes came to me. The broken heels were not a manufacturing defect but a result of wear and tear; nevertheless, they were returned for replacement.

The height of bad behavior was when an irate, shouting customer from fancy Sutton Place called, saying her dinner guests had just arrived, and she had the wrong soup cans. She wanted Vichyssoise, not onion soup gratinée. This was clearly an emergency. My solution was to send an employee to her apartment with the correct soup. When the offending cans came back, to my surprise, they were empty.

The notorious Mr. Huff ran the operational side of the business. He was everywhere in the store, and constantly in motion. We all lived in fear of him.

A rule was that if you noticed a big-time shoplifter from posted mug shots, you called the protection line number—111. I observed such an individual, made the call, and assumed I would be getting the $100 reward for catching the guy.

Even though I was receiving minimum pay, a DS was considered as an executive. Little did I realize the rule was that the nearest sales associate received the money.

In my case, the nearest associate was in the cheese department. To show his appreciation, he gave me a three pound bag of assorted fresh cheeses. I learned to love Danish Tilsit. A bonus was, the smell of the cheeses meant a private seat on the subway ride home.

CIVIL SERVICE PROVES CAPITALISM WORKS

When I came home from college in 1956 and 1957, I worked (as many did) for the neighborhood USPO over Christmas, handling the overflow. I was assigned to a specific postal carrier, and the job was to sort mail in one of the high-rise apartments in Parkchester where I resided.

The carrier kept a few pieces of mail for himself to hand deliver. These were where he had a high probability of receiving a Christmas thank-you tip. I believe I was given four hours to delivery everything to residents in the building, and completed it in approximately two hours. I told the carrier, and he scolded me for finishing too quickly.

He said to come with him, and we drove to Van Cortland Park. We went to a parking lot filled with mail trucks—their drivers were taking their daily unauthorized afternoon siesta.

In 2010, fifty-three years later, I decided to become a US Census taker in Phoenix, Arizona. The pay was good, and I believed I was performing a civic duty, given the importance of the census as it was used to fashion policy. I passed the entrance exam, and then mysteriously, I had to drive all the way to Apache Junction—a distance of fifty-five miles—for a week of open book training. Everyone in my group passed, but we all had questions that went unanswered.

How, for example, do you get inside a gated community when taking the census voluntarily? Why is the census still recorded in paper form? And lastly, and most shockingly, whatever the resident said, you had to write it down without questioning the answer. If a man answered the doorbell and I asked if he was male or female and he answered female, that was what I had to write down.

After training was completed, the last step was to drive another thirty miles to get fingerprinted. It's now January 2023, and this trained census taker has yet to make a single census call.

Leonard Bernstein, photo by Jack Mitchell.

GETTING PAID LISTENING TO THE GREATEST MUSIC IN THE WORLD

Thanks to my step-cousin and neighbor, Stanley Good-man, I worked P/T at Carnegie Hall while attending NYU. As violinist Isaac Stern said, "Everywhere in the world music enhances a hall, with one exception: Carnegie Hall enhances the music."

The Golub Bros. controlled the concessions there, and my first job to work the coatroom. Coatroom checking was a free service, but the genius of Golub's was to start me with six quarters, prominently displayed on the counter. I can't recall a single instance where I was not paid at least fifty cents.

From there, I graduated to the refreshment counter at the dress circle, or mezzanine level, for philharmonic orchestra performances. It was a bit tricky as the patrons could not hear you setting up during the performance. If any noise was made, you were subject to immediate dismissal. It was a simple set up and clean up for the fifteen-minute intermission. We served overpriced orange drinks in a plastic container and pastry before the bell rang.

I listened to the great conductors of the time: Eugene Ormandy (Philadelphia), George Szell (Cleveland), Herbert von Karajan (Berlin/Vienna), and New York's own Leonard Bernstein. It wasn't, however, all classical because monthly there were Midnight Jazz Concerts.

My final gig was as a waiter in the bar and coffee shop. Among my customers was the flamboyant super star himself, Leonard Bernstein, who went on to do *West Side Story;* as well as Dakota Staton, riding high with her hit album *The Late, Late Show;* and Ahmad Jamal, *At the Pershing.* Celebrities never tipped, but I didn't—I was in the presence of music royalty.

The one fringe benefit of this job was a woman on the 8th floor in the apartment building across the hall who, with the shade down, teased us all by getting undressed and waving at us like she didn't care we were watching.

WAITING TABLES IN THE
BORSCHT BELT: ALL-OUT WAR

As in the celebrated Amazon Prime award-winning series *The Marvelous Mrs. Meisel*, NYC Jews often went to the Catskill Mountains in the summer (also referred to as the Borscht Belt, or the Jewish Alps). In my experience, a precious weekend in the Catskills was not all that glamorous. Dad left work Friday before 5 p.m. and the traffic on Route 17 north, where it went through a tiny town that had one stoplight, was the only way to go at the time because the New York State Thruway was under construction and jammed. That single traffic light backed up traffic all the way to the Big Apple Rest. I learned a good collection of curse words from my father as he sat in this backed up traffic.

Somehow, even after all the delays, we arrived in time for a late dinner. All of the major hotels had the same basket of services: the number-one rated Grossinger's, the Concord, and Kutchers, all of which were known for the volume of food provided. That Saturday, we did eighteen holes of golf, dinner, and a show with a featured comic. This was where a lot of big-name comedians got their start, including Sid Caesar, Jackie Mason, Buddy Hackett, Don Rickles, and Henny Youngman. On Sunday morning, we started an early round of golf, had an enormous brunch, and then made the dreaded drive home.

Years later, I had a short stint as a waiter at Schenk's Paramount, thanks to the Stark Employment Agency run by my neighbor Ben Stark, who was in the Navy with Dad. The cultural shock of going from guest to waiter is startling. As a waiter, you eat different foods, have shabby quarters, and there is no mingling with the guests.

I often pushed hard for tips, making nice-nice to the most demanding and obnoxious guests. At lunch time, when every imaginable food was on the menu, I would race from one end of the kitchen to the other filling orders. As a novice, I had the worst station—the furthest distance from the kitchen. I had to hide the best silverware and onion rolls, both of which were in short supply, because tip size was a function of how well you accommodated the guests in this highly competitive environment. It was dog-eat-dog place!

PART THREE

FUN AND FROLIC

"I have a conviction that a few weeks spent in a well-organized summer camp may be of more value educationally than a whole year of formal school work."

— Charles William Eliot

Trail's End Camp for Boys and Girls.

SECTION 14

SUMMER IN THE POCONOS

My parents felt it a necessity for this young Jewish boy to get away from the NYC summer heat—it never occurred to me that they needed private time for themselves. So, at age ten, I went off to Trail's End Camp, located in Beach Lake, Pennsylvania, in the heart of the Pocono's, for eight weeks.

Trails End was pricey in the 1950s, but the camp owner, Joe Laub, delivered a terrific, carefully monitored product. There were Friday night services, supervised lake swimming, a campfire area for roasting marshmallows, an infirmary (mostly for poison ivy), a series of Lincoln Log–styled bunks on the hill (separated by age and gender), a kitchen floor you could eat off, a first-class bakery, three meals a day (plus afternoon snack at the apple orchard, chocolate milk if you were lucky, and picnic lunches).

There was also horseback riding, a rifle range, a recreational hall, a theater, an arts and craft center (where you could make more than lanyards), and most importantly, ball fields galore. These included softball, touch football, basketball, tennis, volleyball, archery, and a golf driving range.

Counselors were all college-age students who got free room and board, evenings off to go almost exclusively to the Beach Lake Tavern, and one weekly day off (going, on occasion, to Joe Biden's Scranton or Monticello). At the end of summer, parents would tip them too—sometimes serious money, as in hundreds of dollars.

The most fun part of this camp was color war, where the camp was divided in half and points were scored on everything from a counselor volleyball game to a waiter dropping a tray. In time, color war was replaced by the Olympics, reducing the pressure on individual camper performance.

There were also individual awards for athletic performance and behavior. On more than one occasion, I won an award for Best All-Around-Camper. The most impressive thing is that when campers arrived on the first day, all of their belongings arrived in a packed trunk that was neatly unpacked and organized within the bunk assigned to you.

I stayed at Trail's End for ten summers, climbing up the ladder from camper to counselor-in-training (CIT) to personal waiter for Joe and Gert Laub, and finally, tennis counselor. At the end of each year, there was a decorative bunk plaque designed by counselors with the names of all kids and counselors. Uniquely, I attained the status of being a camper *and* counselor in the same bunk. I believe it was bunk six.

It's important to note that Joe and the staff went to great lengths to make certain all rules were obeyed, including no smoking, a strict curfew, a morning reveille bugle call, a flag raising, and there was no tolerance of violence. The most exciting thing we did all summer was sneak a Schmulka Bernstein salami into the bunk for a late-night snack for all to share. It was a great summer when our salami total reached one a week.

The summers always flew by. At closing ceremonies, all cried to the song "We May Never Meet Again." To make things less sad, there was a yearly reunion in Brooklyn where most of the campers lived. In time, Brooklyn gave way to the five towns in Long Island, but the reunion location never changed.

Neil Sedaka

I LAUGHED AT THE PANSY MUSIC HEAD AS HE DIDN'T PLAY SPORTS

Every summer, the music and drama department performed a musical in 1956 it was *Guys and Dolls,* and I had a bit part, and I couldn't even sing in the shower. When the curtain came down to a standing ovation, along with flowers for the musical director. We all disliked him because he had no interest in playing ball and chasing pretty girl counselors. His name was Neil Sedaka. While we were wasting our time hoping to become great athletes, Neil was on his way to stardom.

Neil began as a classical pianist at age nine .He studied at the prestigious Julliard School of music. His hit songs written and performed in the late '50s and '60s included: "Oh! Carol" dedicated to friend and neighbor Carol king, "Calendar Girl," "Happy Birthday Sweet Sixteen," and his biggest hit, "Breaking Up is Hard to Do." In 1983, Neil was inducted into the Songwriters Hall of Fame.

Years later, I watched him perform solo for the first time at a theater in Miami Beach. After the show, I attempted to go backstage to see if he remembered me from camp. (We were both born in 1939.) I presented the gatekeeper with a note for Neil that simply said, "Trail's End Camp."

He was kind enough to see me, and we talked briefly about his one summer at camp. Afterwards, off I went, thrilled to have seen him but not certain if he really remembered me.

Lesson learned form this: focus and practice, practice, practice is necessary for achievement in any field. How do you get to Carnegie Hall? Practice, practice, practice.

GIRLS HAVE ALWAYS BEEN MUCH SMARTER THAN BOYS

In my pre-teens I sat next to Bonnie Grey on an evening horse drawn hayride. She was kind of pretty, smart, and very sure of herself. She was far more worldly than me, although we were the same age. Bonnie was just out of my league. We may have kissed each other once on the cheek, and when camp ended, we promised to write and see each other at the reunion.

Upon reflection, I realize she was my first girlfriend. Bonnie's letter arrived and it was long, full of feelings and observations. Her penmanship was as perfect, as was her grammar. What was I to do? How could I possibly respond. I decided I couldn't because I had nothing to offer. So, I "chickened out."

In those days, I was very shy in front of girls, and the movie *When Harry Met Sally* was years away (1989) from playing in movie theaters. The movie explores whether a guy can have a girl as a friend and nothing more. I came from the old school, where if you were a man's man, you had guy friends only.

I went to a dance at the recreational hall, which had music on the phonograph. As was typical, girls sat together on one side of the room and boys on the other. No one moved for what seemed like an eternity. While I was shy, I had learned dancing at the Arthur Murray Dance Studio (where all students were told they had natural rhythm).

Out of sheer boredom, I finally built up the courage asked a girl to dance; she surprisingly said yes. We were early into our dance, and I was about to begin my dip move when by accident, her horse-hair crinoline dropped to the floor.

What was this shy boy to do? I turned tail, that's what I did—taking the easy way out. It was not my finest moment.

AUGUST 1ˢᵀ SWITCH

By the time I became a counselor, females had become a priority. There was a high turnover of counselors from year to year, eager to look at the new crop of staffers. Predictably, the females who were unattractive in July became beauties by August—hence, the "August 1ˢᵗ switch."

In the 1950s, men were as horny as ever, whereas the opposite sex played "hard to get." The challenge, as always, was how to get past first base. Within the camp there were several options for attempting this, the best being the rifle range mattresses used for shooting in place, and behind the rec hall, where it was pitch black. I managed to get to third base once, but I was mostly a singles hitter.

It was not uncommon for counselors to fall in love and get married. Rosalie Steur, a local from nearby Wilkes-Barre, married Stu Sherman, the swimming instructor, who lived in my bunk. University of Vermont fraternity brother Jimmy Showstack from Wakefield, Massachusetts, fell in love and married Marilyn Rubin, who like me had graduated from camper to counselor.

Adrienne, who had big boobs, was a striking female. As a senior camper, she was one of my tennis regulars. Most of the girls came to tennis to hangout and dry their hair, but not Adrienne. One day, I was at the net hitting balls to her on the baseline when one of her returns hit me right in the private parts. I went down in severe pain and Adrienne didn't quite know what to do—help me or leave me. She elected to run away.

When she became a Counselor in Training (CIT) she fell in love with a fellow counselor—a big dude—who was in dental school. I believe they married.

PARENTS DO
THE STRANGEST THINGS

The first parent's weekend of the season was after the second week of camp. As a counselor to their kids, it was fun to match them up—I confess to being most curious. The affluent parents arrived early, lining up at the gate, and then charge to squeeze their children began. I realized we had a big responsibility, so we were very understanding of their concerns. Parents wanted private time with us. Most of the time it was short and sweet, though sometimes there was surprises.

One mother went to great lengths to explain she and her husband would be traveling to Europe. She said that while most kids received weekly phone calls at assigned times, this would not be possible. The solution she gave me was a stack of pre-posted letters. I was to drop a letter in the mail weekly, without the child knowing. Then, when mail arrived, her child would be happy. The mother, to ensure compliance, promised a large tip at end of season.

One camper walked in his sleep. At first, we laughed, then we were concerned he might hurt himself and wondered if his parents were aware of this issue. Turns out, the parents were aware but didn't tell the camp in advance. The kid's mother said it was because sending her child to Trail's End was important to her and critical to her child—he loved camp.

There were three counselors in our bunk, and we all agreed to keep the sleep walking episode quiet. There was little risk of something bad happening, and the camper in question was really a good kid. We moved his bed to the safest location in the bunk and watched him closely at night.

We decided not to bring this up with his parents unless they initiated the conversation. It turned out to be happily uneventful and we hoped, as some of the literature suggested, that his sleepwalking would go away as he got older.

One of my boys, Sandy, had large breasts, was not athletic, and was constantly being laughed at. I talked to his mother and this time elected to be proactive. I learned she had wanted a girl not a boy, hence the name Sandy.

The end of camp arrived without incident. I hugged the kids and said goodbye and told them I'd see them next year.

Funny aside—on my day off, I told one of my kids I was going to visit my parents—they were golfing at the nearby Wayne Country Club. The campers found it difficult to accept the concept that counselors could have parents, even though we were only about eight years apart in age.

SIX DEGREES OF SEPARATION

What started out as a tale of horror, mysteriously ended with a unique Trail's End reunion of sorts. Some believe everything happens for a reason, while others believe in the "Six Degrees of Separation" theory that states every person is connected to another person through a chain of acquaintances with no more than five intermediaries.

A while back, I received what turned out to be a scam call that to me sounded very believable and worthy of checking out. A stranger got on the phone and explained that my grandson, Henry, had asked him to call because he had been in an automobile accident that he caused and got a DUI. He didn't want his mother (my daughter) to know. Further, he had retained legal representation and the other party agreed not to press charges if I wired money.

To make matters more convincing, he put who I thought was my grandson on the phone. He sounded just like Henry. I said, "Let me think about it. Call me back in fifteen minutes."

I called my daughter, and she didn't answer, so I decided for the first time to call her law firm. Her married name is Lauren Eisen, and she is a partner in a family law practice in Rockland County named Rodgers, Habas, and Eisen. I reached the office and said I needed to speak to my daughter and it was an emergency.

I was advised by her paralegal that she was with an important client in lower Manhattan and could not be disturbed. So, I left my name.

I later found out that putting a child on the phone is a common scam. In playing back the conversation, I realized the caller never said Henry's name. Scam over.

This is when the story takes a turn toward the six degrees of separation theory. Lauren's paralegal had gone to Trails End Camp, and my daughter, who was a camp counselor there for one year, didn't realize this. The paralegal had married Alan Laub. Owner Joe Laub had two sons, Alan, who was the oldest, and Michael. I was a few years older than Alan but we had spent time together at camp.

When I was visiting my daughter in Nyack, New York, she had friends over for a gathering. I was surprised to see Alan there and we spent quite a while talking and reminiscing. We couldn't stop—there were just too many war stories to go around.

"You kind of took it for granted around the Yankees that there was always going to be baseball in October."

—Whitey Ford

Jimmy Cannon

SECTION 15

TOY DEPARTMENT OF LIFE

Jimmy Cannon, the legendary *New York Post* sports columnist, said it best: "Sports is the toy department of life." I was hooked on sports from the moment Dad took me to Yankee Stadium—The Cathedral of Baseball—to see our neighborhood team, the New York Yankees, in 1947 when I was eight years old.

A big problem of rooting for the Yankees was that they never lost, and so it did not prepare me for life's ups and downs. (I was, and still am, a fan of the Yankees, Knicks, and Rangers.) I raced home from P.S. 102 just in time to catch the

New York Giant's Bobby Thomson's home run on October 3, 1951, sinking the hated Brooklyn Dodgers. It was known as, "The Shot Heard Around the World."

Growing up in Parkchester, there were no grass fields, so as a result, we played stick ball on the handball court. You got a home run if you cleared two walls and Macy's parking lot.

We also played lots of hoops. I was not very good until I reached age thirty-five, and then I proceeded to play club ball until I reached sixty-six years of age.

Important for my legacy: I made my last shot of competitive play by scoring a three-pointer thanks to Arnie, who was guarding me while cheering me on.

The young kids asked, "Why do you still play hoops at such an advanced age?"I would respond with one of two answers: shut up and play or I never get a high five from my wife.

I was also a good tennis player with a lefty slice serve, soft hands but no strokes. If the opponent didn't have big topspin, ground strokes was an annoying tough out.

James Monroe High School

JOE CAMERON, THE MOST COLORFUL PLAYER ON THE TEAM

Although I had a poor foundation in grammar, I had a passion for sports. Because of that passion, my English instructor and faculty advisor Ms. Marens selected me to as the sports editor of the *Monroe Mirror* monthly newspaper for James Monroe High School, made famous by Hall of Fame Detroit Tigers first baseman Hank Greenberg. I called the column "Here's How."

Monroe had an awful football team. They'd lost the annual Thanksgiving game for twelve consecutive years to powerhouse DeWitt Clinton. Clinton, unlike Monroe, had the advantage of recruiting athletes from outside their district. The best players were tackle Charlie Negron, running back and friend Billy Morgenthal, and Joe Cameron (a fan favorite).

I was elected to interview Cameron, and he was most engaging interviewee I'd had. I opened the column with the following line: "The most colorful player on this year's team is Joe Cameron." Colorful referred to his personality, not the color of his skin—which, by the way, was black.

Joe loved the article as did Ms. Marens. It's sad to think that if I wrote it today using the same words, cancel culture would come after me.

I'm happy to report I was active in the Civil Rights movement, and have had numerous African-American friends. Contrary to what current day culture would lead you to believe, there's not a prejudiced bone in my body (although my lefty friend Last Line Joe accuses me of being an internal racist).

I would have preferred to receive a varsity letter, but the best I could do was playing third singles on the handball team. I lost in the borough championship to a player with one arm (normally a handicap, but not in this case).

My first paid writing assignment was as a stringer for the *New York World Telegram* and *Sun* was calling in the results of games to the Zander Hollender High School Sports Editor. The job paid $7 per game. I didn't resume writing until 1999, forty-three years later.

Cardinal Timothy Michael Dolan

ONLY IN AMERICA CAN A CARDINALS FAN BECOME AN HONEST TO GOODNESS CARDINAL

In my critically acclaimed 2021 two-part publication *Saving Baseball,* part one details the greatness of the game on the field. Then, part two laments the inability of the marketing types to sell the game, as the NFL has now become the new American pastime. On page 51, I introduce the reader to Cardinal Timothy Michael Dolan, who in 2009 became the Archbishop of New York, serving 2.5 million American Catholics. The *National Catholic Reporter* says Dolan has conservative values and a charismatic media personality.

Dolan, a big baseball fan, says most significantly that "baseball is good company." He is a big Cardinal's fan, and vividly remembers sitting with his dad and grandfather listening to the radio on May 13, 1958, when his hero Stan "The Man" Musial got his 3,000th hit—a milestone at Wrigley Field in Chicago.

The Archbishop wrote me the nicest letter, telling me how much he enjoyed the book and, naturally, his mention.

Jerry Lewis fools with the wrong guy.

SILENCING THE KING OF COMEDY

In 1971, as a result of my connection with the new movie release of *H.R. Pufnstuf,* I was selected to be a member of the Hollywood Stars versus a team of retired LA Dodgers in a two-inning exhibition at Dodger Stadium. I dressed but never played.

Our captain, who batted himself first, was Jerry Lewis, nicknamed the "King of Comedy." Lewis starred with crooner Dean Martin in the comedy team of Lewis and Martin. They were widely popular from 1946 to 1956, before Lewis went solo. Lewis was also a philanthropist, becoming the National Chairman of Muscular Dystrophy and hosting their telethon from 1966 to 2010.

Jerry often said, "I've had great success at being a total idiot." When he faced the 6'6" ex-Dodger and All-Star RHP Don Drysdale, this was proved right yet again..

To start the game, he did his routine. Drysdale was not a guy to fool around with, even in an exhibition. During his career, Drysdale had 209 wins and 2,486 strikeouts, entering the Hall of Fame in 1984. Drysdale believed the home plate belonged to him; "I hate all hitters. I start a game mad and I stay that way until it's over."

It took Don less than a minute to flatten Lewis, changing his expression from smile to scared shitless. No one in our dugout liked Lewis because he went out of his way to tell everyone he was the captain and would bat first, so we all enjoyed this immensely.

Victor Seixas and Tony Trabert

SPORTSMANSHIP AT THE DAVIS CUP DOESN'T PAY

I was introduced to tennis at summer camp and then became a fan of the Davis Cup—a premier international team event in men's tennis that was founded in 1900. The United States has dominated the competition, winning 32 titles, followed by Australia with 29. Professional tennis, where athletes play for prize money, didn't begin until September 1972.

I went to Forest Hills in the early 1950s with my friend Stephen Weiss, taking two subway trains and purchasing grandstand tickets for a very modest amount. The courts were grass, the tennis balls white, the rackets wooden, the clothing white, and the players white. Back then, it seemed very normal.

The crowds were small and well mannered—there was clapping but no shouting or booing. We watched America's best doubles team Victor Seixas and Tony Trabert win at doubles. Steve caught a ball that went into the stands and those in attendance encouraged Steve to throw it back, which he gladly did. We were youngsters doing the right thing.

After the matches, on our way out, we saw a concessionaire selling used Davis Cup tennis balls. This was our first look at capitalism at work.

Steve and I are both die-hard Yankee fans, and had been to Yankee Stadium many times, often bringing our baseball gloves in the hope of catching a ball so we could get it autographed. It was unthinkable to would throw those balls back. In fact, fans were willing to risk life and limb to take the ball away from other fans also intent doing the same thing.

The closest I ever came to catching one of those precious balls was sitting in the right field grandstand during batting practice, The ball landed in the next seat, falling on a woman's lap who had her dress spread. I thought for a moment about reaching over and grabbing it, but that would *not* have been the gentlemanly thing to do.

Tracy Austin had talent from a very young age.

TENNIS PRO: BEST WAY TO GET BETTER IS YOGA

I was a member of the Calabasas Park Tennis Club located in the San Fernando Valley West of Los Angeles. The club had 18 hard courts, most with lights, and a center court with stadium seating suitable for tournaments. I watched a match there with Tracy Austin, age 12, and she destroyed a woman six years older than her, who hit the ball much harder, moved better, and had a much bigger serve.

Club amenities included a snack bar, locker rooms and proximity to the lake, which was a perfect jogging length. The major annual event there was a Pro-Am doubles tennis tournament with a draw on Friday night to match the top-teaching tennis pro with the lowest-ranked member.

Prize monies raised were in excess of $5,000, which was enough to attract the best pros in the area. They included Swen Davidson, Trey Waltke, Dean Martin's son Dino, and our pro Sam Match. The rules: a single pro set, best to six, four-point games, with no ad scoring, and the pro would get only one (instead of two) serves to the amateur. Between the money and the one serve rule, the pros were very serious—hence, there was a lot of pressure on the members to play well.

My pro was average, and I was a good club player but nothing more. We won our court, or first round match, on Saturday morning. As was customary, we amateurs bought our pros their lunches. Over lunch I asked the pro for any suggestions to improve my game, assuming we would be talking about strokes and strategy. Instead, he advised I take yoga, which I thought at the time was a religious experience. I didn't ask for further information, because I was afraid to sound ignorant.

Confused by the answer, I performed poorly in the afternoon matches and we went quietly. Oddly, his advice turned out to be an omen that took a while to manifest.

Twelve year later, at age forty-eight, I was still playing club tennis on the clay courts of New Jersey. I had a scary moment one day, based upon an incorrect blood test that indicated a high probability of cancer. Fortunately, cancer was not found after an extensive series of X-rays administered by a doctor friend (and tennis buddy) who went out of his way to be thorough.

I became stressed and anxious and was advised by a co-worker to take yoga from Nicolle Mode Parisian in nearby Garwood, New Jersey. The classes were awesome. There were no other men, of course, because yoga was not viewed as aerobic or competitive, so men avoided it. For me, though, it was just what I needed. I finally learned to relax, and how to lie on my back with my eyes closed without falling asleep.

I am still taking yoga, and my wife—an ex-dancer—became a certified Yoga instructor in 1990. She specializes in restoration, primarily targeted for senior citizens. Geri the Yoga Princess has a big following, among them men too!

Jerry Van Dyke, king of the home court advantage.

GRAND SCALE TENNIS CHEATING BY MY CELEBRITY NEIGHBOR

I resided at 4621 White Oak Avenue in fashionable Encino, California, on the right side of Ventura Boulevard. On my street were a host of celebrities, including Jerry Van Dyke, David Cassidy, Jimmy Webb, and Aretha Franklin. A Calabasas tennis friend—everyone's friend—Ken Harnett introduced me to Jerry Van Dyke, my next-door neighbor. Jerry had two prized possessions: a Macaw parrot and a pristine tennis court.

In the 1970s, well before he played Luther Van Dame in the hit TV situation comedy Coach, Jerry was an actor and comedian and the younger brother of the multi-talented Dick Van Dyke. Most of his gigs were on cruise ships, where he entertained with singer John Davidson. When in Encino, we played tennis on average once or twice a week before conditions became unbearable.

There is an old joke about the Plotnick Diamond, the most beautiful diamond in the world. The good news is that the quality of the stone is genuine, and the bad news comes with Mrs. Plotnick. The same is true for playing Jerry. Having a tennis court steps from my home, complete with refreshments, was great—but Jerry was the ultimate tennis cheat.

I was the better player, but we were extremely competitive. While a bit of cheating is acceptable with no referee calling lines and foot faults, the savvy cheater is generous on all calls except when the point is critical. Jerry, however, was the only one who kept score. Somehow, when he announced the score, he'd added a win for himself and subtracted one for me!.

My wife Geri met Jerry's first wife, Carol, a few times under very stressful circumstances. Carol would knock on the door with the pretext of looking for her Macaw, but in reality she was escaping from Jerry on those rare occasions when he became a violent, nosy drunk.

TENNIS: A GAME
PLAYED BETWEEN THE EARS

The Mountainside Indoor Tennis Club on Route 22 was a short drive from my residency in Watchung, NJ. It ran open-tennis tournaments on Sunday afternoons in the winter, you just had to pay a fee of $25 for a reserved court, a can of tennis balls, and there was a trophy for the winner.

There was no attempt to rate players in this tournament. You arrived hoping for the best competitive match possible. One of the nice things at Mountainside was that you could sit in the upstairs lobby with a clear view of the courts below.

On this Sunday, my opponent was a good-looking young guy. I was probably 25 to 30 years his senior. His honey was in the lobby, and he was looking the part of a stud tennis player, all muscular with long curly hair to impress her. He was wearing Le Coq Sportif attire, and had a large tennis bag filled with 4 or 5 of the latest mid-sized rackets that he probably strung himself.

We warmed up, and he was showing off for his female companion. I smartly used the warm up to determine a strategy. I decided to take pace off the ball and pressure his second serve by standing close to the serving box. His gal motioned to her wrist, indicating she was leaving and wanted to know what time she should return. He signaled with his hand 45 minutes, which was most disrespectful.

I, of course, destroyed him in about 90 minutes. He threw, then broke his racket and refused to shake hands. He disappeared into the locker room to cool off afterwards.

Having fun, I went up to the lobby, told his girl he had lost and suggested she take it easy on him because he was a much better tennis player than me, but he must've lost his concentration thinking of her beauty.

George "The Iceman" Gervin

"THE ICEMAN" IS NO MATCH FOR
ME IN GAME OF H-O-R-S-E

I had a full-time consulting assignment in San Antonio, far away from Geri and Charlie, who were still back in New Jersey. To maintain my sanity, I went daily to the Century Club to work on my shooting. I became a gym rat, wearing my trusty white head band. I was always looking for a game, but sometimes an empty court was the best I could do.

One evening, at the far court I watched an accomplished player drop one basket after another. Never to be overwhelmed, I walked over and asked if I could join. He he said, "Be my guest."

The player was none other than George "The Iceman" Gervin, who was voted one of the top 75 greatest players in

NBA history in 2021. He played for 24 years, accumulating a career scoring average of 26.2 points per game. His nickname was "The Iceman," because he played at such a high level without sweating.

He most amazingly used the backboard, going high off the glass at angles that seemed to defy physics. Even more astonishing was that he could shoot from the deep corner, also off glass—what seems like a physical impossibility.

I began seeing George regularly at the club. To spice things up, I never played him one-on-one (he was a towering 6'7"), but suggested the traditional game of H-O-R-S-E instead. In this game, the first one to spell horse via missed baskets loses. The rules are, if the previous shot went in you have to duplicate the shot using the same technique and identical spot on the court. I decided to forget about all the games George won, and concentrate on the two games where I was victorious.

Back in the 1930s, the two-handed set shot was the rage and in the late 1940s, I started using the two-handed heave to reach the basket. Eventually, the two-handed set shot gave way to the jump shot popularized by Kenny Sailors. But for a game of H-O-R-S-E, I used the pull-back two-handed shot.

George had never seen anyone shoot such a shot, and for my two precious wins I was in the zone: one step back set-shot after another. George's hands were too big to grip the ball that way. George, being a gracious and class act, gave me a moment I will never forget.

The only thing i had in common with slick
was i wore a headband.

MOVE OVER "SLICK" WATTS

Microsonics was a company started to market an invention that added sound to a children's book. The company was based in Century City, LA, and owned by Sam Schulman. Sam was also the 1967 founder and President of the NBA Seattle Supersonics. They relocated to Oklahoma City in 2008, and were renamed the Thunder.

The Supersonics were a championship caliber team in the 1970s, earning the championship in 1979 behind HOF Coach Lenny Wilkens and star players Gus Williams, Jack Sigma, and Paul Silas. As anyone who watched NBC's sitcom *Frasier* knows, the team owned the city.

Sam was a delightful guy, and like me, a New Yorker. He graduated from NYU. I met him for the first time at the prestigious tennis club in Palm Springs. I believe we played doubles on their grass courts.

I traveled extensively for Microsonics, charging hotel rooms with my Seattle Supersonics identification card, photo included. My favorite Sonics player was "Slick" Watts because not only was he the first to lead the league in steals and assists, he also wore a head band that was a carbon copy of mine.

One day when I was checking in to the Ambassador Hotel in Chicago, I found myself in line with "Slick." We shook hands and talked hoops for a few minutes before he went up to his room. When I approached the desk, I showed my ID and the clerk, without looking up, said, "You know, by the way, I'm a big fan of the team. Thanks for staying with us."

John Lucas

NO LONGER WAS I
'MONEY' FROM THE CORNER

When I was on a Houston consulting assignment, I stayed in a rented corporate apartment. It turned out I was in sports heaven as I also got to be a member of the Westside Tennis Club. The club had 36 courts covering all the surfaces: red clay, hard-true, and grass (where I lost handily to Zina Garrison in an exhibition), hard courts, and indoor courts.

The tennis pro there, John Lucas, was my hero. He was a fellow lefty and a college All-American at Maryland, who also played and coached in the NBA. (John also had a drug addiction which he overcame.)

The basketball program was what really turned my head. I played on the club team. I was the last player selected against stiff competition who had paid a high entry fee, but we had Coach Lucas who gave me minutes, and his 15 year old son, John Jr., who had a great shooting touch.

Jr. went on to Oklahoma State, getting to the final four for Coach Eddie Sutton. Jr. then had a brief stint in the NBA, but he was too small and didn't have an NBA body like his father. Senior contended he could have become a top ten tennis player though.

The basketball set-up was second to none, as it was the training facility for the Houston Rockets. There were multiple NBA courts, a locker room with training tables, and a gigantic whirlpool bath, which I was frequently allowed to use when it was unoccupied.

The NBA had a lockout from July 1, 1998 to January 23, 1999, causing the season to be reduced to 50 games. Many players came to our facility during the lockout, as the Rockets were the only team where NBA players could practice.

I was on the court with many stars, and when they needed someone to fill in, I was Johnny-on-the-spot. One day, I was sitting on the bench and during a scrimmage they called me into their huddle. This is when 6'9" Antonio McDyess reached down, put his hand on my head, smiled and said, "We're going to run a play for you." I was, after all, "money from the corner" and that was to be the play.

Sam Cassell passed the ball, Chris Morris set the screen, and I squared up and took the shot. The ball barely hit the rim, and I was devastated. Fortunately, the guys laughed, gave me a game ball, and I got lots of high fives.

Just like comedian Rodney Dangerfield said,
"I don't get no respect!"

EARNING RESPECT:
MORE IMPORTANT THAN WINNING

When I was in NYC for Toy Fair, I needed a basket-ball fix. So, with a free pass in hand I went to the Reebok Sports Club/NY on Columbus Ave. at 67th Street. To my disappointment, one of the two NBA regulation basketball courts was down, so the wait to play was close to unbearable. But when you need a fix, you put up with the nonsense.

Per usual, if your team lost, you went to the back of the line. Winners stayed on, and players in order of arrival waited on the sideline and shot foul shots to form the new and opposing team.

I was 30-plus years older, shorter at 5'9" and slower,than the rest of the players there. Plus, I could only go left—I was a lefty. When it came to shooting foul shots, though, I had an 85 percent average. The Guinness World Records shows Ted St. Martin as the foul shot record holder with 5,321.

When I stepped to the foul line, four of the five players had been selected, and the fifth was to be decided between me or the 6'6" African-American guy who could dunk front and back. Back in the day I was often asked if I could dunk, and I had a truthful pat answer: I never tried!

No one was cheering for me, just as in *The Great Santini* starring Robert Duvall, and there were about 50 guys hanging around. My opponent, feeling sorry for me, went to the three-point line to give me a fighting chance.

I said no thanks, and matched his five shots. A few in the crowd began rooting for the old white guy with a head band. My opponent finally missed and the crowd urged me to go to the foul line and take the win and play. That's not who I am. I went to the three-point line and missed. He would go on to win, and I went to the dreaded treadmill. As I left, I received an ovation.

In 2017, I was a guest on the PBS Radio Show *Only a Game* co-hosted by Bill Littlefield. The show ran in 264 markets on Saturday mornings for one hour. It was a magazine style show for the serious sports fan, and I was there to promote my latest sports book, *Greatest Sports Finishes of All Time*.

I went to the local studio and Bill and I talked for about an hour. I thought it went well. I didn't even look at my spread out note cards!

When the show aired, Bill had edited my segment down to seven minutes. Instead of focusing on the book, he was more interested in why I wrote the publication and spent most of the time on one specific event—the event described above.

FEAR LEADS TO MY RUNNING
IN WORLD RECORD TIME

I began jogging in LA during the height of the running craze. *Runner's World Magazine* was launched in 1966 and had built its circulation to more than 500,000, the NYC Marathon was now big-time with prize money for winners, and runner Jim Fixx's 1977 book about the health benefits of running, *The Complete Book of Running,* was a big seller. (Fixx would later die unexpectedly while running in 1984.)

One time, I had the funniest experience jogging with Geri early in the morning. An LA cop gave us a ticket for jay walking while jogging.

On business trips to Taipei Taiwan, I would jog each morning—with only a room key around my wrist—to Madame Chang Kai-Shek's palace. She was the first lady of the Republic of China. Once outside the city limits and heading in the direction of the palace, there were Taiwanese soldiers who were at parade rest, with their rifles loaded and bayonets fixed.

They were on high alert, since they feared the communists on the Chinese mainland could attack at any time.

In 1981 I had taken a job in NYC, and my family was back in LA (until our house sold). I was staying at the Warwick Hotel on West 54th Street near Sixth Avenue, just below Central Park and its 6.1 mile running loop.

While many joggers had been mugged there, I was not afraid. It was a late summer Sunday evening and the sun was shining brightly.

As I entered the loop, I realized I might have been the only jogger in the park. I heard bongos being played from one side of the park to the other—like they were communicating with each other. My imagination got the better of me and I became afraid, thinking the gangs would be waiting for little ole me to come jogging by.

I became so terrified that I ran my ass off, achieving my best running time—perhaps even a world record. I arrived back at the Warwick dripping wet 30 minutes before my business dinner appointment. Yes, fear is a natural motivator.

"Hey, Ralph," said Bill Morgan, "this... is going to be a tight one after all."

"Right," said Ralph Carpenter, "the opera ain't over until the fat lady sings."

This was said about the Aggies, who rallied for a 72–72 tie late in the SWC tournament finals and was reported in the Dallas Morning News *on March 10, 1976: This was the first use of this phrase reported in the media.*

SECTION 16

ZAFTIG

Back in the '80s and '90s many people were engaged in novelty new product development, looking for next hit license like: Star Wars, Ninga Turtles, Cabbage Patch, Strawberry Shortcake, The Smurfs, etc. Count me among those chasing that elusive license. My candidate was the phrase "It Ain't Over 'Til the Fat Lady Sings." The origin of the phrase is still being debated, and it is in the public domain; therefore, it's probably not available for licensing usage.

There, however, was a chance and I took it. I had preliminary artwork of the logo done, the Fat Lady as a Superhero, and a crack trademark attorney working a stone's throw away from the trademark building. He was a big sports fan, though with the NHL he rooted for his home team, the Washington Capitals, while I was for the Broadway Blues.

In a miracle of sorts, I was granted rights. While the saying could be utilized by anyone, if it went on a product (say a cap or T-shirt) they would be in violation of my rights. Importantly, rights need to be exercised or they go away, so calendar pressure was real.

I had a partner who was moonlighting as a freelance graphic designer and I bought him out once the rights were secured. I now had an array of artwork that branded the Fat Lady as a sports Superhero. I added a musical jingle with a female opera singer breaking glass, and I was ready to do battle.

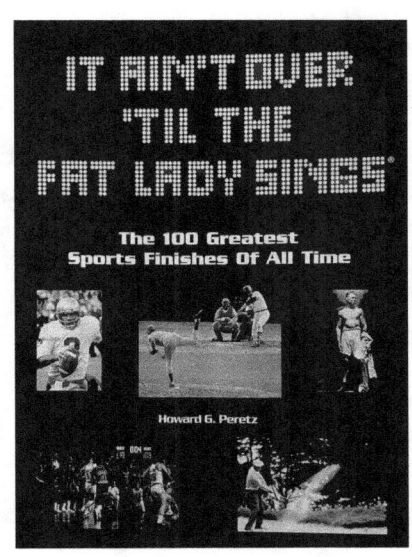

BOOK AUTHOR BY ACCIDENT

book, once upon a time, was considered a key first licensee deal, and Harper & Row agreed to publish a book titled, *It Ain't Over 'Til the Fat Lady Sings: 100 Greatest Sports Finishes of All-Time.* Frank Fochetta was a fellow Jersey guy and a VP at the publisher, managing the Special Markets Division. Most of the growth in publishing at the time was merchandising books through non-traditional channels. For example, books on flowers to florists, books on wine to liquor stores, and naturally sports books to sports retailers like Sports Authority (which later became Dick's Sporting Goods).

Frank as they say was my rabbi, the individual on the inside pushing the *Fat Lady* book forward through the system. Suddenly Frank's duties changed and my title seemed destined for the dumpster. This, even though compilation books at the end of the century were widely popular (it was 1999).

Frank did the smart and honorable thing by bringing the *Fat Lady* to Barnes & Noble, which had its own imprint. I met their editor, Frank Hoffman, and loved the concept. His loyalty to the New York Mets caused me some second thoughts, but this life-long Yankees fan sucked it up and behaved accordingly. The scoreboard cover, which I hated, was mandated and images of the fat lady were to be minimized while emphasizing the phrase.

A royalty deal was industry standard, but with one big catch: I had to do the writing. While I have much to say, I knew little about the rules of this particular road. I had a poor foundation in grammar. I mean really, what the hell is a parallel structure or the difference between an adverb and a pronoun?

The contract provided a substantial advance against future royalty sales, enabling me to retain the services of a book packager. Packagers do all the heavy lifting, much like subcontractors building a house. One last complication was that I took a full-time consulting job with DSI, which was headquartered in Houston, Texas—far away from NYC's publisher's row. There was FedEx and book galleys went back and forth, so all deadlines were met. Father's Day 1999 was the release date.

IF ONLY THE FAT LADY HAD BEEN THIN, NOT ZAFTIG

Having Barnes & Noble as a publishing partner had many advantages: your title would appear in the front of the store in special displays in approximately 600 stores in the United States, retail prices were much lower than selling through the archaic distribution network, and all stores were eager to do author book signings. The offset is the chain would not spend a penny on marketing, which was left totally to the author. Also, of course, sales were restricted to B&N outlets—there was no internet or Amazon at the time.

It is worth noting that when I did a personal store appearance, books flew off the shelves. This book did well enough to justify a second printing, which was released Christmas of 1999.

The book was part of a major marketing/licensing effort, so I needed a good NYC-based sports marketing agency. I found a one in National Media Group (NMG), headed by Michael H. Goldberg.

Importantly, Michael believed in the *Fat Lady* and we entered a royalty sharing arrangement. NMG would provide office space, public relations support, and arrange for meetings with high profile promotional partners in return for their cut.

Michael had nothing but style. He wore a different handmade bow tie each day, and was a health nut—he walked to work daily, swam every workday morning, was a tea gourmet (white tea his favorite, because it has the most antioxidants). Since sitting is bad for your back, he also had a standing roll-up desk.

Michael knew all the sports movers and shakers from his days at the ABA as legal counsel. He was a driving force behind the merger with the NBA.

My favorite client of his was the Major League Baseball Players Association (MLBPA). The assignment seemed on the surface to be rather ordinary, but in reality players resisted attending trading card shows and signing autographs, even though they were contract obligated. NMG had to send account executives to the players' homes and drag them to the airport, then hold their hands for the balance of the engagement.

Fat Lady PR placements were numerous. There were many newspaper stories, including one paper that gave the book a john (toilet) rating of ten. The book's biggest break was a two-column spread with a picture of me caressing the book that ran in *USA Today*.

I did many radio shows too, although I never did get on "Mike and the Mad Dog," which was the number-one sports talk radio show in the country at that time. The favorite gig for this life-long Yankees fan was a radio interview at Mickey Mantle's restaurant on Central Park West in NYC.

The interview was at the front of the establishment and beyond me was the bar, where I could observe Geri sipping a glass of champagne. Back then, hearing your name on the radio was a big deal, When I got in my car after heading home to Jersey, I heard the broadcasters thank me for the interview, and then make one last plug for the book. As actor and writer Spalding Gray said, "There are only a few perfect moments in one's life, and the key is recognizing the moment as it happens." I did, and this was indeed a perfect moment.

Michael had pushed for a major meeting and the big day finally came for the *Fat Lady*. I was dressed to the nines, with full-sized Fat Lady character cutouts, a mixed musical jingle, books to distribute and a PR scrapbook. I was on my game.

The audience of 10-12 individuals was sitting at a U-shaped table with the head-honcho seated in the middle. My pitch was directed at him. Ten minutes into my act, I could see he was not moved. Instead of going on as planned, I stopped and said out loud, "Why are you guys so uninterested?"

The answer was, "We don't like the Fat Lady character because she's fat." I realized then that the meeting, for all practical purposes, had ended. So, on my terms I did a Jack Parr—I walked out while delivering a few choice words.

First, it was impossible for the Fat Lady to be thin. Then, I briefly mentioned popular fat performers like Rosie O'Donnell who was my daughter's neighbor in Nyack, New York. She once hugged me and I disappeared into her breasts. Also mentioned were Rosanne Barr, the animated Fat Albert cartoon, and the popular artist Botero who painted large women and made them so appealing.

There was, however, good that came out of one of the low points in my business career—I went on to become a self-published author, writing mostly sports books. This is where I became recognized as the Old School Sports Junkie.

Ralph Branca and Bobby Thomson a few days after Thomson hit the "Shot Heard 'Round the World."

"THE FLYING SCOT" LIVED NEXT DOOR

In my 2018 publication *Fat Lady Greatest Sports Finishes of All-Time #1*, I talk about "The Miracle of Coogan's Bluff." This was when New York Giants player Bobby Thomson nicknamed, "The Flying Scot," hit a walk-off home run at bottom of the 9th on October 8, 1951, at the Polo Grounds. This defeated their hated rivals, the Brooklyn Dodgers, 5-4.

Thomson's three-run homer came off Ralph Branca, wearing #13, and pitching in relief of starter and ace Don Newcombe. Interestingly, Thomson had played centerfield but moved to third base to accommodate rookie Willie "The Say Hey Kid" Mays, who was the on-deck batter when Thomson went yard.

There was controversy surrounding the home run. Branca claimed the Giants had stolen the sign, and Thomson said it was just a bad pitch. They later became good friends and close business associates, and appeared together for speakers fees that went on for decades.

Fat Lady sports trading card collectible products were created to celebrate the 50th anniversary of the sport, featuring a grouping of 100 retro cards capturing the entire 1951 season. They were presented in a collector's tin designed by Todd Radom early in his career. Today, Todd Radom Design is acknowledged as the leading sports team logo creator.

With prototype presentation in-hand, I took Todd with me to The Fleer Company in Philadelphia. Fleer was a leading trading card manufacturer founded in 1895 that was acquired by Upper Deck in 2005. Fleer loved the concept and assigned their senior designer to work with us.

The push was on to meet the marketing date of October 8, 2001. Both Bobby Thomson and Ralph Branca were scheduled to be present at the planned introduction. Sadly, the program was canceled due to the horrific bombings of the World Trade Center on September 11th.

Shortly thereafter, Thomson invited me to his home in Watchung, New Jersey. I lived just down the road in the same town. He couldn't have been more gracious. We even had lunch in his dining room.

After lunch he took me on a home tour. I was hoping to see a plethora of sports memorabilia but there was none to be found. I was tempted to ask why but I respected his privacy.

BETTER THAN WIFE'S COOKING

I grew up Jewish in a Kosher household. My grandma was a "Food Nazi," much like the Soup Nazi in *Seinfeld*. This meant I didn't get to go to a restaurant until I could sneak out. It was a very special treat.

My first recollection of dining out was the food counter at the neighborhood F.W. Woolworth. I had a BLT accompanied by a root beer float, both of which I gulped down. No too long after that, in nearby St. Claires, I had a hot fudge sundae and the soda jerk made certain that the fudge overflowed.

My parents took me to the Chinese restaurant that was within walking distance of our apartment on Sunday nights when we didn't have deli—either way I won. It was a typical Chinese meal: wonton soup, egg roll, spare ribs, chicken chop suey, and most importantly, the fortune cookie at meal's end.

As an adult, I became a foodie. I am never afraid to venture out and eat something out of the ordinary like escargot, alligator, uni sushi with quail egg, mutton, and octopus. I was living in NYC, the restaurant capital of the world, so I had lots of great choices. Side note, the first restaurant on record was located in Paris in 1765. It was a soup kitchen opened by one A. Boulanger.

After getting married, Geri and I moved into a railroad apartment on a sublease at $135 per month. It was located in the Murray Hill section of Manhattan—136 East 36th Street. Our plan was to dine in every eatery on 36th street, working our way from York Ave. on the east side west to 12th Avenue. We never made it further than Fifth Avenue.

Armed with an expense account, I did a lot of business during lunch, which was sometimes referred to as a "power lunch." I have had the good fortune to work and travel most everywhere, and we were excited to find new restaurants on our own.

I turned 48-years old in 1987, the same year that my father passed away. This is when I changed my eating habits for the first time. Since Dad died unexpectedly of a heart attack, high cholesterol was considered the bad guy at the time. So, I eliminated red meat from my diet—no more roast beef end cuts, Beef Wellingtons, T-bone steaks, filet mignons, or even burgers at Jackson Hole. Happily, Fuddruckers partially filled the void with their ostrich burgers. My diet grew even more restrictive once I was diagnosed with cancer at age 66.

It had become apparent that a lifestyle change was needed, and at the suggestion of the wonderful Marie Hardenbrook, I went to a lecture in Scottsdale, AZ, where I formerly resided to hear Dr. Peters of Mind, Body, Medicine. I went on a very tough diet that excluded any food that came from a parent. This included fish and chicken, and dairy.

Dr. Peters also believes all sugar is bad. He thinks the body is unable to distinguish between sugar from a fruit and processed sugar, so fruit was off the table too. My wife and I argue about sugar all the time. But, as a result of diet and chemotherapy, I am cancer free—the best two words in language. I am also off statin drugs and anti-depressants. That means, in my book, I win the argument.

Once I turned 80, I became a bit more social and have become a cheating vegan. I remember reading *Chicken Soup for the Soul* years ago and recall the author writing about an 80-year-old woman who was asked what she would do differently if she lived life over. She said, "I would have eaten more ice cream."

As to my occasional cheats today, they are very tame but exciting to me—grilled chicken, sushi and broiled fish, plus French fries, the only allowable fried item. How long can an individual live on a diet of beans?

My best friend, Milan Mermall, and I go out weekly on Thursday and now Friday for lunch. We have been doing it for over twelve years. Milan is an authentic foodie who lives to eat. By contrast, I eat to live. For dessert, we play a hand of liars poker.

EVERY SAUSAGE COUNTS

Luigi was a typical local neighborhood high school pizza hangout. James Monroe, our High School on Burke Avenue, was a block from the Elder Street 'L' station. We loved pizza because it was a sharing food and cheap. Plus, it was fun to have learned how to fold a slice, as the cheese oozed down. Could life get any better?

On this night, there were four of us to share an eight-slice sausage pizza. We all began counting the number of sausage pieces on each slice, and found they were uneven. Picking up sausage pieces and moving them around the circular board game not an easy task. We decided the best way to handle this was to raise our fists. The waiter was smart enough to solve the problem by taking the pie back to add sausage and count them so they were evenly distributed, averting a Sausage Showdown.

NYC does have the best pizza. My favorites were: Amerigo's and its perfect waiter Guido, Rocky Lee, The Original Ray's Pizza, and Joe's in the East Village.

Naturally, there are great pizza places throughout the country that I have frequented, including Casa Barbi on Commonwealth Avenue in Beantown; Wings Bar pie in Norwood, Massachusetts; Chicago's Lou Malnati's deep dish Chicago-style with its patented butter crust; Pizza Peddler in LA's San Fernando Valley; and the chain California Pizza Kitchen, which started in Beverly Hills and was the first to feature exotic toppings like barbecue chicken. Here in Phoenix, my favorite place is Oregano's.

RETIRED BASEBALL PLAYERS
ON THE MENU

Al Schacht's "Score Card" Restaurant at 102 E. 52nd Street opened in 1942 and lasted until the 1960s. Al was the third base coach for the Washington Senators from 1924 to 1934. He was known for his humorous antics, earning him the title of "The Crown Prince of Baseball."

Al brought this sense of comedy to his establishment too. They had an oversized baseball menu, and at the bottom of menu it read, "Where the screw balls meet." Most significantly, the dishes were all named after old players: Dizzy Trout, Connie Mackerel, Pepper Martin Steak, Zake Wheat Cakes, and Chicken a la Clyde King. Dad took me there when I was most impressionable.

A CELEBRITY RESTAURANT WITH THE CELEBRITY ON PREMISE

*J*ack Dempsey's Broadway Restaurant*, which moved from across Madison Square Garden to the Brill Building between 49th and 50th Streets (1935-1974), was known for two things. First, Jack "The Manassa Mauler" Dempsey the former Heavyweight Champion was always on premise (not feasible today). The second was they had the best New York cheesecake according to many.

It seems like yesterday when Dad introduced me to Dempsey, the greeter and maître d'. He seemed much bigger than 6'1" and 187 lbs., and he had the firmest handshake of anyone I had ever met, before or since.

He was among the most famous athletes of the first half of the 20th century. On September 22, 1927, he had a rematch with Gene Tunney. The "Long Count" drew 150,000 to Soldier Field in Chicago and was heard by 50 million radio listeners worldwide. It was referred to as "The Greatest Fight of the Century."

Orsini brothers really cared. Armando Orsini, right, and his brother, Elio, started Orsini's in 1953.

PROSCIUTTO CRISIS

O rsini's, open from 1953-1984, was on West 56th Street. It was my restaurant of choice, and my selection for a pre-Toy Fair kickoff dinner. It was my first as head of marketing for Hasbro. Restaurant critic Gail Greene said one goes to Orsini for the food, like it is theater, so I thought it was a good choice.

Companies worked all year to get ready for the March Show. Actual orders were written and sales were tallied daily. The year's business was determined by these three weeks in March, so the stakes couldn't be higher.

Permanent showrooms at the Toy Building at 200 Fifth Avenue had been under design and construction for months. These were often one-of-a kind prototypes that were highlighted in display cases and demonstrated by airline stewardesses working the show in their spare time.

I hardly slept as we got things ready. I was busy putting out fires daily, but I never anticipated a restaurant crisis. I got a call from the owners of the very trendy Italian-style café, Armando and Elio Orsini. They were so upset and emotional because there was no prosciutto to be had for the prosciutto melon that was on the menu. In one of the most important decisions in the history of the fair, I said to go with the shrimp cocktail—disaster avoided.

Jacqueline Kennedy Onassis

NOTORIOUS GUEST UNDRESSED MY WIFE WITH HIS EYES

Sign of the Dove was a celebrated Upper East Side restaurant that Jacqueline Kennedy Onassis, referred to as her favorite. Affectionately known as Jackie O, the widow of President JFK, liked the ambiance, which was perfection. They had large flowery menus that did not contain prices when given to women—a very nice touch.

Back in 1967, Geri and I were invited by the Hassenfeld's (Hasbro's founding family) to dine there and meet special guest Marvin Glass. His company was headquartered on La Salle Avenue in Chicago, and he hated travel because he was afraid to fly. So, this was indeed a special occasion.

Marvin started the toy invention business and manufacturers eagerly awaited a call that would indicate it was show time for them. His toy credits included Mr. Machine, Rock 'Em Sock 'Em Robots, Evil Knievel Stunt Cycle, Mousetrap, Operation, and Lite Brite. While the industry trend was qualitative research with children, Marvin said no to this practice. His opinion was: kids can only see what's in front of them, but I can see the future.

Marvin was a womanizer and his stories were legendary. After dinner on our taxi ride back to our hotel, I asked Geri what she thought of Marvin. Geri said, "For the first time and only time in my life, a man undressed me with his eyes." Marvin clearly had good taste in both toys and women.

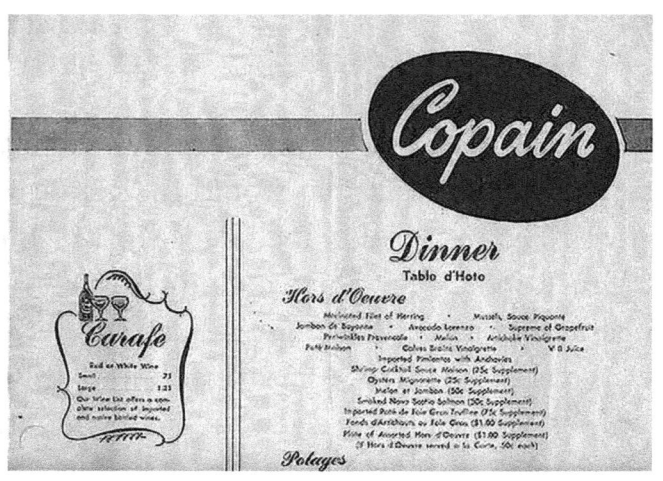

A RESTAURANT SAYING
THANK YOU AS YOU ENTER

The Copain, a bistro, opened in 1945. It was located on York Avenue in Midtown Manhattan, and was made famous worldwide by the 1971 academy-award winning movie *The French Connection*. FBI agent Jimmy "Popeye" Doyle, played by Gene Hackman, was on stakeout across the street as French drug kingpin, played by Fernando Ray, dined inside.

We locals marveled at the cuisine. We were also most appreciative that when you were being seated, there was a reservation holder with a dime enclosed, thanking you for making the reservation call.

Jimmy, seated at La Grange.

KISS ON THE HAND: JUST A PART OF THE SHOW

Jimmy's La Grange at 151 East 49th Street was in reality a stage on which host Giulio Prigioni performed his magic. While seating you, if there was a lady present, he kissed her hand. He also described the entrees for the non-existent menu, and explained the house specialty—Chicken Kiev (pronounced Kee-ev). He would drawing on the tablecloth how the meal was prepared, and when the main course arrived, he used his knife to split the Kiev so the garlic butter filling would spill out on the plate.

It was almost as good as sex. No wonder it was featured in one of *Mad Men's* Emmy award-winning episodes. I was in the advertising business in the 1980s and *Mad Men* was authentic in every way: wives were hidden far out in the suburbs, while ad men played during and after work.

Best steak in town, but it's in a high risk neighborhood

WENT TO PETER LUGER
STEAK HOUSE TO STEAL

Peter Luger Steak House was established in 1887 on the Brooklyn side, below Williamsburg Bridge, and was regarded as the best steak house in America. Part of the excitement of going to Luger's began in the parking lot, which was small and poorly lit in what appeared to be a high crime area.

Inside, it was all about working your way to the T-bone through a gigantic wedge of all green, no yellow, lettuce smothered with large dollops of Roquefort dressing. Many years earlier, I went to pay my bill with an American Express card I was shocked to learn they don't take third party credit cards. I solved this problem quickly—I applied for and received a Peter Luger credit card.

On this occasion Rod White and I were principals in a small New Jersey gift manufacturer called Starshine. Our guests for the evening were Suzy Spafford and her EVP, who was formerly a school teacher. Suzy was the founder and creator of Suzy's Zoo, a greeting card line with whimsical and happy characters. We had just become their exclusive stuffed toy licensee.

All of Suzy's drawing translated easily into stuffed toys. The star was Suzy Ducken, a cross between a chicken and a duck. Her cards did well in the Western US, but not as well in the on the east coast where everyone in the business was oh so serious.

Getting ready to depart, Suzy said, "Do you mind if I leave with a piece of Peter Luger dinnerware?" showing me the large handbag she was carrying that was appropriate for the caper. We agreed, and on subsequent visits, the caper was repeated. Because the stuffed toy line was most successful, she ended up with quite the dinnerware collection.

RUDE AND UNHEALTHY
TRUMPS BIG EASY CUISINE

Carnegie Deli gets my vote over Stage Deli for best New York deli. (Carnegie has the better cream cheesecake; hence, my vote.) They have similar menus and proximity, the same style, identical rude wait staff, tables that are too close together, and each claims to have the best pastrami. The two establishments are constantly trashing each other.

One of my clients at the time was United China, located on Tchoupitoulas Street in New Orleans. They were most hospitable. We stayed in the French Quarter at the charming Maison Dupuy Hotel. We also dined at the best places the city had to offer: Brennan's, Commander's Palace, Antoine's, Felix's Restaurant, and Oyster Bar. While I loved po boys, beignets, and oyster pie, the banana Foster pie at Commander's is my favorite dessert of all time.

The President of United China was coming to NYC for a trade show and I asked him to pick a restaurant—price was no object. To my astonishment (happily for my pocket book), he said the Carnegie Deli. As predicted, the wait staff was surly, telling you, among other things, what not to order. We also shared a table with other guests—no privacy whatsoever.

On my last look at my guest as we left, I saw he was all smiles with pieces of corned beef stuck between his teeth.

MAKING THE SALE AT THE MOST BEAUTIFUL RESTAURANT

C afé des Artistes, located just west of Central Park on West 67th Street, is the most beautiful restaurant in town thanks to the six murals painted by building tenant and renowned artist Howard Chandler Christy. It was the perfect setting to impress Uta Brauser, a young artist from Florence, Italy. I had met at her booth at the Javits Center, where she was presenting her sculpture collection of African-American males. The *New York Times* reviewed her work and said it was imaginative, realistic, and forceful. I was hoping she was looking for representation.

Since the German-born Brauser had a fondness for black males, I decided to bring my good friend Alex Shipman along with me. He just happened to be African-American and was very nice looking and spiritual to boot. Alex was my wife's tennis pro, although they chatted more than they hit tennis balls.

I remember when he bought us a large mushroom for display in our refrigerator. I also played tennis with Alex and he had immaculate strokes but hated playing me, as I had a knack for playing defensive tennis.

Like most tennis pros, Alex was poor, so a night on the town at a fancy restaurant where he got dinner and got to meet a talented and striking woman was an easy sell. I explained the mission and Alex delivered. He dressed appropriately and ,with flowers in-hand, he was most attentive and, of course, kissed her hand.

I did get to represent Uta but unfortunately never made any money. I couldn't get her to sculpt famous black athletes like Michael Jordan. It was not her thing. Hallmark Cards, where I was well connected, first said let's do it, but ended up passing—not an uncommon occurrence.

As an aside, I couldn't explain to Uta, who was very sharp, that flying from NYC to Hallmark headquarters in Kansas City cost more than her flying from Florence to JFK, so she traveled at her expense.

CREATIVE WAY TO GET A FREE PRE-THEATRE MEAL

Café un Deux Trois was founded in 1977 and is located at 123 West 44th Street, just east of Broadway Theaters. They specialize in French Bistro cuisine. The restaurant promoted its prix-fixe pre-theater menu priced at $145 per person. You also needed a reservation at 6:30 p.m. or before to guarantee you'd make the 8 p.m. curtain.

We had a party of four— two couples—and when the clock struck 7:15 p.m. we had yet to be served. I had already begun drawing with the provided crayons on the white paper tablecloth, writing in large text for everyone to see, "The service sucks!"

The maître d' observed my artistry and elected to comp the dinner. The meal was still served but it was rushed, and we arrived at the theatre on time. With the surprise dinner savings, rather than putting the money in the piggy bank, after the theater we went for a night cap to hear the legendary American cabaret singer and pianist Bobby Short perform at the Café Carlyle where he appeared for thirty-five years.

RUSSIAN NOT SPOKEN HERE

The Russian Tea Room was opened in 1927 by dancers from the Russian Imperial Ballet. It was our location choice for our daughter's birthday dinner. The decor is art deco and it was designed with one-of-kind tiffany lamps. The restaurant is just 20' wide between, as it's sandwiched between two towers on 57th Street next to Carnegie Hall. After dinner that night, we had tickets to see singer and song-writer Arlo Guthrie, the son of legend Woody Guthrie, known for social protest lyrics and his hit City of New Orleans, first recorded in 1972.

To make the birthday special, I called in advance to order a birthday cake with the words Happy Birthday Lauren written in Russian on the top of the cake. The woman answering the phone said, after a few seconds of silence, "Sorry, no one speaks Russian at the Russian Tea Room."

How could this be possible? I wondered, but then again Haagen-Dazs ice cream was made in the Bronx and Burberry raincoats were manufactured in Baltimore. But still, in a famous café where Warner LeRoy of Tavern on the Green fame reportedly spent $36 million to fix up the joint, you would think they would hire just one individual who spoke Russian.

HOSTING A REHEARSAL DINNER: PARTY STRESS FREE

Marchi's was located in a step-down restaurant town house on street level at 251 East 31st Street, and was my personal NYC favorite. It operated for 90 years before closing in 2019. We were there this time for a Friday evening rehearsal dinner for daughter Lauren and her husband-to-be David. The wedding would be the following evening at the Puck Building.

The food was Tuscan-style and the entrees were always presented in the same order: antipasto, homemade pasta, a fish course, two mains (chicken and veal), and two desserts. It was a leisurely dinner and you felt like you were dinning in a fancy warm home aided by the well-behaved German Shepard who had his place near the kitchen in full view of the guests. In 2019 the cost for the prix fixe dinner had increased to $61.75 per plate.

For us as the hosts, it couldn't have been easier. This was a no fuss way to deal with the rehearsal dinner. There was no stress about what to order and no variation in price among the guests.

It is sad that Marchi's closed. Apparently, a leisurely dinner is no longer in vogue.

SINGLE FRIED HOT DOG WORTH CROSS-COUNTRY AIR TRIP

R utt's Hutt, founded in 1928, is located in Clifton, New Jersey, and is world famous for its deep-fried hot dogs. They were named #1 hot dog in America by the *Daily Mail*. The establishment is so well-known that when a new highway ramp was built, it provided the Rutt's Hut with a cutout.

At the time, I was consulting for Proll Toys, a small domestic musical instrument manufacturer. The company president was Marty Huff, an accountant by training who married Susan Proll, who elected to devote her time to raising her family but came in part-time to handle collections and put out fires. Her brother Peter handled production but had little appetite for business expansion and risk-taking. Susan was by far the smartest family member.

I was asked to find an international sales representative when the company agreed to shift production to China from Bloomfield. The switch was essential to doing business worldwide. My recommendation to fill the job was based in Los Angeles, but was a former New Jersey resident.

He agreed to fly east on his dime if I bought him fried hot dogs at the Rutt's Hutt. After he stuffed himself, we went off to Proll headquarters for a face-to-face introductory session. We were just getting started when Susan barged in to discuss a mundane credit issue. After Susan left, the candidate loudly asked, "Who is that f$*!ing c$*#t?"

Well, that was the end of that interview! I immediately showed him to the door, and we had a mostly silent ride to Newark Airport. As he left, he said the hot dogs made the trip worthwhile.

DIVORCED COUPLE UPSTAGES CHIPPENDALES DANCER

After a day of consulting work, I played a set of tennis with client Marty Huff of Proll. Per usual, I played client tennis and then went out to a neighborhood Italian eatery. Near our table was what we thought was a typical sweet sixteen party—but it was not.

It seems the parents were divorced, and the husband's job was to provide the entertainment and take videos. When it came to the fun part, the husband obviously listened to the daughter with no input from his ex-wife. On cue, a Chippendales dancer showed-up, began doing his thing as the overjoyed girls watched. The mother, on the other hand, went ballistic.

Words were exchanged, the ex-wife broke the camera. The horrified girls watched as the ex-husband defended himself, all the while using very colorful and inappropriate language. Instead of a relaxing business dinner, we ere treated to a carnival side show.

Years later, when I was at Starshine a Gift Company where I was one of the principals, I signed an exclusive licensing agreement to market Chippendale teddy bears. They were adorable and more importantly G-rated. They had a single blade of hair, a white collar with a bow tie, and black boxers. The bears sold like hot cakes at Chippendales' Shows, a few of which I attended in person.

The opportunity, however, was to achieve broad gift distribution. We showed the item with much fanfare at the National Stationery Show at Javits Center in New York City. There I stood next to a Chippendales dancer. We had huge crowds but not so many buyers.

In the middle of the second day of the show, a young, attractive woman came over to me and said, "I'd rather have you than him. I just love your baby blues."

I was flattered, and asked, "Do you really feel that way?"

She responded by saying, "Do you see that guy standing over there? Well he gave me ten bucks to say that." So much for my ego boost.

BEST NOT TO ASK

Paul's Kitchen was an authentic, small Chinese establishment in City Market Chinatown, located on San Pedro Street in Los Angeles. It opened in 1946. The food was well prepared. It was wallet friendly, and while Chinatown has all but disappeared, Paul's Kitchen lives on.

As it says on its website, "Veteran Chinese Restaurant dishing out chop suey amid Dodger Memorabilia." In the '70s, I was a regular customer because I was working at Olympic Boulevard for Regal Apparel. They specialized in matching men's coordinates from different Asian factories.

My wife's parents, the out-laws, were retired and residing in Palm Beach, Florida, in a community that had a golf course—something at the top of their bucket list. After many requests, in-laws Sylvia and Sam decided to stay with us at our home in Encino. To get there, Sam would be flying for the first time.

His first words on arriving at LAX were, "Where is the earthquake damage?"He had seen the news coverage of the devastation from the February 9, 1971, San Fernando Quake that measured 6.6 on the Richter scale. I told him the only damage remaining was in my head.

Sam loved fresh fish, so off we went to Paul's Kitchen. Sam had quite an appetite that evening. That changed though when he asked what kind of fish he was eating. The waiter told him it was barracuda. Sam thought barracudas were most likely poisonous and he suddenly got pale. I told him barracuda is not even remotely related to his favorite fish, which is cod. It is a common name for the demersal fish genus Gudus.

We were also fans of Chinatown in NYC. Located in lower Manhattan, was comprised of many restaurants, and all of them were good. I don't remember individual names but we always went for dim sum. My son Michael was eleven when we took him to Chinatown for the first time. He got to battle with a live chicken named Clarabelle. She was known as the Tic-Tac-Toe chicken and was in the fair amusement arcade. Michael didn't know it was impossible to defeat the chicken and to be satisfied with a tie.

Kuda Bux walking on hot coals

SMALL ROOM MAGIC LEGITIMATE

The Magic Castle in the Hollywood Hills was founded in 1989 and bills itself as the most unusual private club in the world. It is home to 500 magicians who belong to the Academy of Magical Arts. I had a contact at Johnny Carson Productions who would get me passes there from time to time. Carson started as a magician in his native Nebraska.

It was so much fun to go there. You needed a password to open the front door, and then to the player piano named Irma played any song you requested. The bartender could also raise and lower your bar stool—something I didn't know the first time I went and wondered if I'd had too much to drink!

Besides the entertainment, they also had a well-priced meal, which you rushed through so you could get to the magic. The magicians who perform in the small rooms were especially good.

Geri and I, enclosed in a small room, sat across the table from an unnamed magician. Geri was given a handful of dice that she held in her hand. The magician then covered her hand with his and asked Geri was if she thought the dice were still in her hand. She said, of course they are. She squeezed them as tight as she could. But, as you probably guessed, the dice were gone when she opened her hand.

Although magic is based upon the desire of the recipient to have the magician succeed, when the magic happens to you the result can't be explained.

The Magic Castle also had a main theater where we went to see Pakistani mystic Kuda Bux perform. His act seems simple enough—guests cover his eyes with dough (I was one of those wrappers) and then cloth covered his entire face.

Audience participants would go up to the blackboard and write words and Kuda Bux would say them out loud. He brought down the house when someone wrote in Russian—he laughed, then said the words in Russian.

I enjoy a good magic show, and I've seen many, including David Copperfield, Henry Blackstone, Siegfried and Roy, Penn and Teller, etc.

ROMANTIC RESTAURANT
LEADS TO TABLE SEX

Ivy at the Shore is a romantic, high-class oceanside restaurant that attracts like-minded couples. On this evening, all seemed normal until a couple, forgetting where they were, put on a show for all to see. It started with innocent kissing and moved on to French kissing, then body touching and finally to the clothes starting to come off.

There were accompanying shouts of ecstasy. And ,yes, all of the guests stopped eating and drinking to watch. The couple was young and attractive, and they were either comfortable in this setting or completely oblivious to their surroundings.

As the two exhibitionists climbed on the table, with the food and dinnerware flying around, the horrified manager who was not trained to deal with this type of thing was finally forced to act. He aggressively moved the couple to an adjoining party room that happened to be empty. He then closed the doors and raised the sound level on the restaurant's background music to drown out any further shouts.

Being savvy, he bought all of us a glass of champagne and a piece of Caramel Cheesecake. Then, he led us in a toast to romance. All of the guests left very satisfied that evening!

EATING BAIT TOO MUCH FOR NEBRASKA PATRON

Matteo's is an iconic Westwood hangout that was founded in 1963. They serve seafood and the wait staff sang in tune and with gusto. This was one of my favorite eating spots in the 1970s.

I had just taken a new position at Mode Furniture as VP of sales/marketing. The new owner of Mode, Bob Fogarty, held court at Matteo's on a regular basis. In addition to me being a new hire, Avery was also recruited as the new financial head and manufacturing type, who specialized in T&MS (time and motion study).

Fogarty, who was trying to impress us, ordered for everyone without taking requests. The appetizer was squid, a delicacy I had eaten many times. I noticed the financial guy seemed a bit queasy as he looked at it, and he appeared to be debating whether to indulge or pass.

At that moment, Avery asked, "What's this on my plate?"

Someone else at the table answered, "Squid!"

With that, Avery, who was seated next to me, actually fainted. When he recovered from the episode, he said that the idea of eating bait was too much for him. He was embarrassed for sure.

Bob Fogarty was a bad guy and I knew it, but a head-hunter friend who was persuasive convinced me to take the job. Plus, I would do anything to stay in LA at that point. On my first day of work, I was given a plane ticket to San Francisco. I was to meet with Mode's Northern California salesman, the longest serving rep. in the company.

My job when I got there was to fire him on the spot. I was then to get back on the plane and come back to LA so I would be ready to meet the Mode sales force the following morning. Fogarty wanted them to fear me.

(Side note: The fired salesman later sued. Apparently, the original owners of the company, the Furiani family, had told him he had his job for life.)

Mode was an awful place to work. Bob's sales growth demands were unrealistic and the pressure was intense. I decided to get out of Dodge, and Bob agreed. The one good thing about my contract was that Bob agreed to pay me while I was out of work. While this might sound like a great deal, being paid while living in the City of Angels, it was not. The problem was my wife and kids had their own schedules, and I was just in the way. Further, when you're not working and are out and about, you spend money.

One final thought on Bob—the arrogant elitist. He was proud of saying: "If you took all the money in the world and redistributed it among everyone, the same people who had the money in the beginning would soon have all the money again."

Natalie Wood

GLAMOROUS FEMALE MOVIE STAR KILLS MY BUSINESS DEAL

At the time, this soufflé restaurant (the name escapes me) was fashionable, and reservations were hard to get. The fact that celebrity sightings were all but guaranteed had a lot to do with this. I judged this the ideal location to meet with my most important client, Rod White.

Rod was the president of New Jersey-based Knickerbocker Toys, the largest stuffed toy manufacturer in the world. (He would later become a close friend and business partner.) At this dinner, I hoped Rod would advance monies on future new products to Package Play Development, the name of my invention company.

I picked up Rod at the Beverly Hills Hotel, and the restaurant was a just short ride away. I gave the car to the valet and we were immediately shown to our table. There were rows of tables for two separated by glass dividers. The tables were wood top and bottom. I noticed immediately that Rod was staring at the female facing him on the other side of the divider, while I was forced to stare at her male companion.

It turns out the couple was the most beautiful in tinsel town: Natalie Wood and Robert Wagner. I learned that Rod had fallen in love with Natalie after seeing her in the 1958 movie *Marjorie Morningstar*, which based on the Herman Wouk novel. This was the first time a Jewish novel became popular and successful.

Natalie, then in her early 40s, amazingly looked better in real life than on the screen. Wagner, her first and third husband, was a good-looker as well. Needless to say, Rod didn't hear a word I said the whole evening.

Many, many months later, while I was at the Estero Beach Hotel on the Baja, the deal finally closed.

WHO WEARS A TIE ANYWAY?

Pinnacle Peak Patio was a Western themed joint that opened in Phoenix in 1957 and closed in 2018, when this once isolated and remote location in thriving North Scottsdale became suitable for development. I arrived in Phoenix in late 1961, and was working for General Electric's Computer Department. My team leader, Pete Scola, who had sent this empty suit wild boar hunting, recommended a visit to this authentic Western dinning spot.

Geri picked me up at work and off on this journey we went. We traveled on mostly poorly marked dirt roads to get there because at the time Scottsdale was just a few blocks wide, though now it has a population in excess of 250,000.

Upon arrival at the restaurant, the host immediately cut my tie. They had a deal where they took the bottom of your tie and attached your business card to and then they would put it up in the rafters. No one at GE told me this form of Western hospitality was going to happen, so I was more than a little surprised and was now down one work tie!

There was a similar custom at Keens Chop House at 22 West 36th Street in Manhattan, which opened in 1885 and is the only business establishment remaining from the once thriving Herald Square Theatre District. Keens collects business cards with pipes from guests for their collection. It reportedly numbers 90,000 now, and many of the pipes make it to the ceiling. Keens is world renowned for its mutton chops.

CHEMOTHERAPY DATE RESTAURANT RECOMMENDATION

Don and Charlies was a sports museum disguised as a steakhouse and ribs restaurant. The food and service were among the best in town. The place opened in 1981, and closed in 2020 when the aging force behind the eatery, Don Carson, received an offer too good to turn down.

Don's memorabilia had a distinct Chicago flavor. It was his hometown after all. The collection featured hundreds of signed baseballs from the legends of the game, along with photos, plaques and jerseys.

I got to know Don reasonably well and he was kind enough to host one of my book author signings. Don was perhaps

ASU's biggest booster, hosting the pre-game football meal for the Sun Devils.

When I arrived in Phoenix in late 2006, I was recovering from a rare form of cancer (orbital) that had spread to my chest. This disease is affectionately referred to as "old man's cancer" and it requires chemotherapy. At that time, before the rules of privacy destroyed patient and caregiver interaction, fellow patients became your loving support group. For example, there was Lillian, who had stage four cancer (mine was treatable, but sadly hers was not). We became friends and worked our schedules so our treatment dates were identical whenever possible.

Lillian had a wonderful spirit. She rushed to canasta once the dripping stopped, and she had a love for baseball that matched my own. Her son was the clubhouse manager for the Oakland A's, and her devoted husband moved into an apartment to be near her.

Lillian showed up one day with an A's World Series ring, her proudest possession. She was so happy when she placed the ring on my finger during one of my many six-hour chemotherapy days.

The first time I went to Don and Charlies, I related the story of Lillian's passing, and out came the champagne glasses. We toasted to Lillian, and I, of course, had a tear in my eye.

"Don't judge a book by its cover"

MY SON HEARD GUEST GO OUT OF HIS WAY TO SAY I WAS A GENIUS

Pappadeux's Sea Food Kitchen is my go-to restaurant in town when I'm hungry, although east-siders very rarely make it to the west side of town. I got hooked on their Cajun-styled fish recipes when I lived in Texas, where the wait for tables was most often close to 90 minutes.

My son, Michael, was in town from New Jersey for my 83rd birthday, and we were joined at the restaurant by Rudy and Michael Kassinger, recent arrivals in the Valley of the Sun. Michael was my son's childhood friend from when we lived in Westfield, New Jersey, and Rudy, along with his late wife, Sonia, were among our best friends.

I had recently written a blank page book titled *Best of Biden*, that is a humorous gag gift. I outvoted both my wife and son, who said to leave the book home—because the Kassinger's are very obviously politically left. I said, "It's my birthday, and besides, the book comes with a gag guarantee."

I presented the book to Michael Kassinger and he laughed out loud—the common reaction to this book. A funny thing then happened. A group of fun-loving African-Americans at the next table asked to see the book. They all chuckled as well, and one of them, smartly attired with a perfectly placed cowboy hat, moseyed over.

His name was David Miller and he turned out to be an investment banker from Wyoming. When he learned I was the author, he shook my hand and said to everyone, "You're a genius."

David claimed he was connected at the highest level within the Trump Organization and he promised to spread the word about it.

I FAILED AT PLAYING
CUSTOMER TENNIS

The Maisonette Restaurant in the Queen City (Cincinnati, Ohio), is located on Sixth Street and is longest running Mobil Five-Star Restaurant in North America. Its run lasted from 1968-2005.

Bernie Loomis, former President of the General Mills Fun Group, and a toy industry innovator— think Star Wars figures—positioned his colleague and friend, Joe Mendelsohn, as the president of Kenner Toys and we were to have dinner. On that occasion, I had been hired as a consultant to make certain that Kenner's product manager, an ex-Proctor and

Gamble employee, didn't screw up his latest pet project: Care Bears' stuffed animals. Before I boarded the plane for Cincinnati, Bernie—who frequently sent me out on assignments—had one request, and that was to tell him everything that went on at the meeting.

As our elegant Maisoneete dinner neared its end, Joe said, "Don't tell Bernie anything we discussed tonight." That's known as being between a rock and hard place.

For years, I avoided playing tennis with Bernie because I was pretty good and Bernie was very much overweight. At a moment of weakness, I agreed to play at his clay court club in Long Island City. Bernie arrived, wearing a warm-up suit and I remember thinking that he looked like a large stuffed bunny.

My strategy was simple: hit the ball directly to the bunny. But after about 15 minutes, Bernie shouted, "Play tennis!" So, I promptly did. That was the last time I ever saw Bernie—no more consulting gigs.

COLLEGE STUDENTS DESPERATE FOR HOME COOKED MEAL

Tau Epsilon Phi is a Greek letter fraternity that has a UVM chapter started in 1919. I joined in the fall of 1958, after suffering freshman year dining on dormitory food. Back then, in many places there were signs that read "NO JEWS OR DOGS ALLOWED," so getting a bagel was never a remote possibility.

The best dinning spot in Burlington, Vermont was at the downtown bus terminal. There was also the Park Café — it was expensive but disappointing.

When I pledged TEΦ, I had no idea the food would be exceptional. Plus, living in the fraternity house was also a treat.

The TEΦ meals were awesome because the chef, Jimmy Kates, a TEΦ lifer. He knew his way around the kitchen and always knew what us brothers wanted to eat. We all wanted lots of comfort food, large portions, flexible hours, and leftovers. My Grandmother would have been proud, even though the only cook she ever truly liked was herself.

BREAKING WATER WINS EVEN
WHEN YOU CAN SMELL DINNER

D urgin Park was part of the Faneuil Marketplace, established in 1742, is one of the oldest restaurants in Boston. It is located in the part of the Freedom Trail that's
considered "The Cradle of Liberty." In keeping with tradition,
the restaurant had communal seating, long tables and a narrow staircase that went from entrance to the dining room.

Back then, I ate red meat and salivated for the roast beef end
cut made famous at Durgin Park. The dish was so appealing
that tourists with large video cameras couldn't resist filming
it. Reservations are not accepted there, so where you stood on

the narrow staircase upon arrival was key to how soon you'd be eating.

On this night, the restaurant was packed per usual and we were looking at a 30-40 minute wait on the staircase. It was torture. I could smell that gigantic end cut of roast beef on the bone.

We were three steps from the top when very pregnant Geri's water broke, so off to the Boston Lying-In Hospital we hurried to have our first child. At the entrance to the hospital, I encountered Doctor Waldo Fielding, who authored the book *The Case Against Natural Childbirth*. It was March, and Waldo, ever the personality, arrived in his top-down corvette convertible, wearing a scarf wrapped around his neck.

Lauren Joy, my baby girl, was born on March 6, 1966. From then on, we were more interested in pictures of Lauren than roast beef.

THE ONLY TIME MY WIFE
EVER GOT WASTED

The Ritz Carlton in Buckhead was a first-class hotel. Geri loved the view from our room, because it was of the Lenox Square Mall and the Saks Fifth Avenue sign was prominent. Geri loved me but probably not as much as shopping. To her, a 50 percent off sign was more invigorating than any energy drink.

I was in town for the Atlanta Gift Show and would be working, so Geri would have time to pursue her favorite pastime. My concern was whether I could make enough money selling toys to cover her enthusiastic purchases.

At the top floor of our hotel there was a four-star restaurant and it had a prix fixe four-course dinner. It included a different wine with each course. Mixing drinks was considered a bit risky, but the Sommelier reassured us it would be fine. Also, our trip home involved an elevator.

Geri barely made it to the elevator. She was having trouble standing on her own and giggled all the way to our room. It was the first and last time I ever saw Geri drunk.

TOUGH BREAKFAST FACING A
SCARY EATABLE CENTERPIECE

I had been to Mexico many times as a tourist—Cancun, Aca-
pulco, Baja—but this was my first business trip there. I was
headed to Monterrey, the steel capital of Mexico. This was
hardly a tourist destination, since it was far from the ocean.

I was starting a new preschool toy development project
with a vendor selected by my client. We were meeting for a
kickoff breakfast at mid-morning. This would be followed
later by a late lunch and then a siesta followed by dinner. The
Mexican culture was more laid back than I was used to.

I was the last to arrive for breakfast and we sat at a large
round table, and there were eight of us in attendance. As
the guest, I was seated facing the eatable centerpiece, which

317

included a barbecue cow's head. I had planned on having bacon and eggs, but this decor made my appetite disappear.

This traditional dish making up the centerpiece was what is called Barbacoa. It's made from the meat of a cow's head, which is cheap and rich in flavor. The cheek is loaded with collagen and slow cooking enhances its savory, silky texture and imparts a lot of flavor. I don't remember anything else that happened for the remainder of the meal but I stayed the course and did not throw up.

For the rest of the trip, I had breakfast by myself in my room.

La Tour d'Argent "Your Duck" serial number card .

SIGNATURE DISH WITH A KEEP-SAKE NUMBERED CERTIFICATE

When we were on our honeymoon in Paris during the summer of 1962, I was determined to dine at the best place in the most romantic city in the world. La Tour d' Argent was the number-one rated restaurant in Paris, according to *Fielding's Travel Guide to Europe,* so that's where we went.

Their prices were steep, far beyond our daily Paris budget for the week's stay. The wife and I agreed we would make a sacrifice for a single night of first-class fun. We were not disappointed.

Tour d' Argent is on the left bank of the Seine, which is a perfect setting. There's an unobstructed view of Cathedral Notre Dame de Paris, which is beautifully silhouetted at night.

The restaurant dates to the 1900s. Frederick Delair started the tradition of presenting a numbered certificate with each pressed duck meal served. Part of the show with this dish is that the waiter brings in the duck on a sterling silver tray for the diner's approval, then returns later with the pressed duck. Upon paying the bill, we received a numbered certificate to commemorate the evening. I'm sure we still have it stored somewhere in the attic.

Since then, I have become an animal rights activist, and pressed duck would be over the top for me now.

CAN FRESH FISH BE TOO FRESH?

Jumbo Kingdom Floating Restaurant located in Aberdeen, Hong Kong, was the best way to guarantee that your dinner included fresh fish. The fish arrives on deck for the guests' consideration before dinner. Once you've decided, the fish is numbered and you take the number upstairs. Once you're shown to your table, you hand the number to the waiter, and voilà the exact fish you chose is cooked and appears on your plate.

While Jumbo Kingdom was obviously for tourists and mainland meals were much better, it was still a moment I'll never forget. There are also the Yau Ma Tei Boat People you pass on your Aberdeen journey. These people, who fish for their living, reside close to shore but *never* leave their boats during their lifetimes.

Side note: Sadly, the Jumbo Kingdom closed in March of 2020 and the floating restaurant ship capsized on June 19, 2022 after leaving Hong Kong.

Witty Repartee

1 **a:** a quick and witty reply

  b: a succession or interchange of clever retorts:
    amusing and usually light sparring with words

2   : adroitness and cleverness in reply: skill in repartee

PART FOUR

WITTY REPARTEE

*Please enjoy this collection of isolated funny
events that require no backstory but are
worthy of being shared and remembered.*

Random fraternity panty raid.

SPENDING A NIGHT IN JAIL

It was 1958 and I was pledging Tau Epsilon Phi at the University of Vermont. During that period, between being recruited and initiation, I was a pledge and subjected to a variety of pranks. None of them were the least bit dangerous, but many were embarrassing. It was all in good fun.

This was well before the sexual revolution and, believe it or not, one of our tasks was to sneak into the girls' dormitory and steal undergarments. This was affectionately referred to as a "panty raid." We did many other silly things, including the olive race, where you crawled nude with a spiced olive between your buttocks; and bombardier, where you lay on your back with your mouth open and a raw, opened egg was dropped into your mouth from a height of approximately 10 feet — the object was to see how far it went down your throat before you gagged.

The prank I remember most vividly was stealing Canadian road signs with French writing on them and bringing them back safely across the border. Montreal, where the drinking age was just 18, was less than a two hour drive from us. I was with three others for this adventure. We were so proud—we liberated six such signs without being detected. This moment of joy was just temporary though. It ended when we reached the small town of Saint-Jean-sur-Richelieu at about midnight and were pulled over by a Canadian Mountie. The signs were found and we were taken to a jail, which consisted of two prison cells.

We were asked to pay a fine to secure our release, but we all were close to broke so we had to spend the night in jail until the money could be wired in the morning. Although booked, we were promised nothing would show on our records to indicate we were ever jailbirds.

Tony Bennett

CROONER PICKUP
OR INNOCENT INVITE?

I was to pick up my girls at the famous Polo Lounge in Beverly Hills. We were dining out and they were having a pre-dinner cocktail. It turns out, the crooner Tony Bennett, of "I Left my Heart in San Francisco" fame, was at the bar and invited them to join him.

In the subsequent car ride home with me, the girls were both giddy, each certain Bennett tried to pick them up.

GETTING EVEN WITH
DR. GORGEOUS

D r. Gorgeous, an endocrinologist at St. Joseph's in Burbank, was one of my best friends. We played tennis frequently, and when he choked on the court, he would say out loud, "Oh, Eddy!"

When he fractured his back in a freak skiing incident, he wasn't on the slopes—his skis became tangled while he was on the lift. He was rushed to St. Joseph's, where the nurses went gaga over him.

Side note: His description of the nurses shaving his pubic hairs before surgery was one for the books.

IMAGINE SLEEPING
THROUGH AN EARTHQUAKE

Mother visited us in LA, and was staying at our ranch house in Encino. On the morning of February 9, 1971, we were awakened by shaking and loud noises. We met in the hallway and I told her go back to bed, which she amazingly did.

Mother was blessed with the ability to fall asleep easily— she even fell asleep in NYC taxi. No wonder she slept through the M6.6 San Fernando Earthquake, which had its epicenter near the Magic Mountain amusement park.

UNESCORETED WOMEN FORCED TO EXIT POSH NYC HOTEL

The elegant Park Lane Hotel on Central Park South has a restaurant and bar located on the second floor. This maximizes the view of the park. I was staying at the hotel with my boss, Fred Adickes, his wife, Susan—who later changed her name to Summer with him—as well her sister, Margaret Gregory.

Fred and I were at a meeting across town and told the women to meet us at the bar. When we got to the bar, they weren't there. They weren't in their rooms either. It seemed very strange.

Later we got in touch with hotel management, who checked and advised that house detectives had escorted the women out of the hotel. It seems the policy there was that unescorted women were not allowed in the bar. They'd been mistaken for prostitutes! This was made even more humorous because Susan and Margaret were among the nicest and most wholesome women you could ever meet.

CREATIVE BIKINI THINKING
BEFORE CREATIVITY

Designer Paul Ishikawa was an exceptional talent, and after much arm twisting, he agreed to work at our offices rather than his home studio. Our offices where in Playa Del Rey, near the beach, and Paul spent most of the day watching the girls in bathing suits go by. But his daily bursts of drawing activity sometimes lasted a half-hour when his creative genius went on display.

When Paul sent directions to his residence, it was always accompanied by artwork: compass, ocean, and plants along the roadway.

JOHNNY CHIANG'S WIFE
NOT AS ADVERTISED

Johnny Chiang's factory in Taichung, Taiwan, was where Hamp bags were fabricated. A Hamp bag was a proprietary laundry bag with a gusset that gave the product the capacity of a hamper. I spent months in Taichung and Johnny was the perfect host. He even invited me to his home.

When I got there, his wife was dressed in traditional Chinese attire and served the dinner. She smiled, but said nothing.

One day, Johnny brought her to LA, and Geri reluctantly agreed to take her to Beverly Hills for the day. It turned out Mrs. Chiang was totally with it and not the silent flower I'd' met. She was fluent in English, stylish, LA knowledgeable, and she and Geri had lots of fun together.

OSU Coach Woody Hayes

HORRIFIED KIDS WATCH DAD CURSE

Business associate Norman Lunenfeld, head of NBC Enterprises, got us reserved tickets to both the parade and the 1976 Rose Bowl. Geri and I and our two kids left early that cold morning. We were looking forward to the game between UCLA and Ohio State.

I was a big Bruins fan and hated OSU, mostly because of their coach, Woody Hayes, who was known for "three yards and a cloud of dust" and for pacing along the sidelines and gesturing to the opposition.

UCLA, without a first down, was trailing 3-0 at halftime. As Hayes went to the dressing room, he gave the finger to the UCLA section. I yelled out a string of curse words at him, forgetting I was in the company of my family. The kids were shocked that their dad would use curse words in public.

My need for cursing ended as UCLA, behind MVP quarterback John Schirra, rallied to upset the Buckeyes 23-10.

I FELT EMBARRASSED FOR THE TOP BANKER

L ittle Lee S., an authentic suede shoe type and an associate of mine, was heading to a bankruptcy hearing where he owed the bank a great deal of money and was signed personally. As the hearing was about to start, Lee pulled up in his Mercedes Benz convertible just as the VP of the bank arrived in the same parking garage. The only difference was that bank VP was in an old Buick sedan. Lee laughed, waved and of course the bank came up empty.

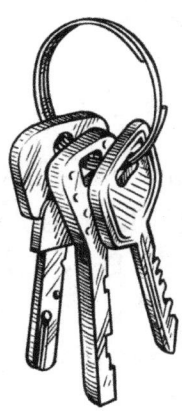

OVERTHINKING

My best friend in New Jersey, Mike Tobin, was a very successful attorney. He was an ambulance-chaser by day and a good club tennis player on the weekends. He was every bit my equal.

Our friendship was based upon being doubles partners; however, it waned when Mike began to beat me regularly and needed to play with someone more competitive. He was committed to winning every point at all costs.

I could beat him because his forehand was prone to errors, and he was inclined to double fault when under pressure. Mike practiced and corrected these deficiencies. I also had some faults, as I lost a bit of my competitive edge when work became so stressful that I went to the courts to hit and relax. For me, every point was no longer a matter of life and death.

Mike frequently bought fresh fruit before playing tennis after work but often left the fruit in the club refrigerator when he went home. He got tired of forgetting the fruit and came up with the perfect mousetrap: place his car keys in the refrigerator adjacent to the fruit. The problem was that Mike, upon leaving couldn't find his car keys, so he called AAA and had his car was towed.

Only when he got home did he realize where his keys were.

MATCHBOX PRESIDENT
IS LAST TO KNOW

S tu Drell, who later would become a cherished colleague of mine in Houston, was president of Matchbox Toys in New Jersey. He wanted me to work for him, so we reached an arrangement where I would run marketing for Matchbox but still continue my consulting practice.

A final hurdle to securing the deal with Matchbox was a courtesy visit with David Yeh, Matchbox owner, and Stu. We met at Yeh's UN Plaza apartment, that came complete with a houseboy. I chatted with David for a few minutes, and surprisingly, he asked me some questions about Tyco. At the time, they were one of my consulting clients.

Stu walked me to the elevator and said, "That all went well. We'll to be in-touch."

The following day, it was announced that Tyco had purchased Matchbox! Stu was out of a job but later we would work together in Houston.

WET T-SHIRT FOR AN ORTHOPEDIC SURGEON

I hit tennis balls regularly with Dr. Ed Rachlin, a retired orthopedic surgeon who got religion and now advocates against surgery. Geri partially tore her ACL and took his advice, and after a lengthy bed rest, is good as new.

Ed loved tennis. He was not much of a player but when he showed up at the Netherwood Tennis Club, I always found time for him at the end of the day. I was pleased to hit balls with him. He was the nicest guy you could ever meet. The only catch was that he didn't run much, and his wife felt strenuous exercise was very important. Solution: I would wet Ed's shirt at the conclusion of our sessions.

Nat "Sweetwater" Clifton

POIGNANT SWEETWATER MOMENT

I arrived at Chicago's O'Hare Airport on a cold winter's night, and needed a cab ride to downtown. I saw an available cab and the name on the medallion was Nat Clifton. The driver was probably was in his 70s. He was a big African-American man and I had a hunch that he had played NBA basketball for my hometown team, the New York Knicks.

I remembered getting his autograph and watching him knock down Adolph Schayes, the star of the Syracuse Nationals. Clifton's nickname was Sweetwater.

When paying the cab fare, I called him Sweetwater and he turned around smiling from ear to ear. We hugged each other. He wouldn't take money for the trip but I gave him a very large tip and thanked him for the memories.

Sweetwater was one of the first three African-Americans to play in the NBA, but at the time the league was struggling to stay afloat, so he was poorly paid.

UPON REFLECTION
IT MAKES TOTAL SENSE

I was an empty suit (square) with an MBA, and at age twenty-one I went on an interview to meet with the president of the Linen Supply Association of America. It was headquartered on Arthur Godfrey Boulevard in Miami Beach. The idea of this New Yorker working in paradise was beyond my level of comprehension and I couldn't wrap my head around why the Linen Association wasn't located in a major market like NYC or Chicago.

I asked the obvious dumb question, "Why are you located in Miami Beach?"

The answer was, "That's where I want to live."

No wonder I didn't get the position.

HOWARD STERN PRE-EMPTS
KEY ACCOUNT SALES CALL

Mike Mott, my street-smart sales rep who later got religion and became a deacon in the church, had arranged for an 8 a.m. "stop and shop" buyer meeting so I could make an early flight out of Boston. He knocked on the buyer's door and discovered he was listening to one of Howard Stern's favorite bits: a girl guest playing music with her vagina in his radio studio.

It seemed unfair that a business meeting was being preempted by such lewd behavior—besides, I was a Don Imus guy. I was invited to join the group and, I admit, we all had a great time. I would see the buyer on my next trip order, as I'd promised.

P.S. It should be noted that Mike had a near death experience. Fortunately, his wife knew what to do and saved him—that's when he met God for the first time.

Lowell, MA

LISTEN TO YOUR SUBCONSCIOUS

I had an opportunity to make a career change when I was interviewed by chance in New Jersey to become the president of a small, well-financed start-up computer software company. I would be reporting to a young, dynamic group executive who loved my blended background of academic excellence and small business consulting.

I was between jobs and consulting assignments, and the pay was good. So, when the job was offered, I smiled and said yes.

There was one further ceremonial step, I had to visit the operation. It was located in Lowell, Massachusetts, 90 minutes northwest of Boston. The objective of this visit was to politely introduce myself to my team of eight and say how much I was looking forward to working with them, shake hands and leave.

I thought I did this task reasonably well, but the boss called me the following day and said he had to withdraw the offer. He said everyone complained that I was much too aggressive.

In reality, my gut said I know nothing about computers, and Lowell, once known as the cradle of the industrial revolution because of its textile mills, was now a small city in decline in the middle of nowhere. My heart won the battle with my mind, another way of saying my subconscious took over and tanked the deal for me.

FROM LUXURIOUS DIAPER CHANGE TO TOP EXECUTIVE

My family visited the Hearst Castle estate, located on 127 acres in San Simeon, California. The castle was a tribute to publishing tycoon William Randolph Hearst. I never will forget the ornate marble-tiled swimming pool, seen in the photo above.

My son, Michael, had to have his diaper changed on the grand piano there. Today, Michael is an EVP with A&E Networks, a cable network owned jointly by Hearst and Disney.

GARBAGE GOES COAST TO COAST

I built my first home in Sharon, Massachusetts. It was the perfect location, halfway between Boston where we socialized and Pawtucket, RI, where I worked. Back in the day, the town was a summer lake community.

The builder, Arnold Foster, was happy to build one-off custom homes and we went contemporary with a deck house for us. It was our first actual home, having previously moved from apartment to apartment.

We moved into the house on West Trail Drive in the summer of 1969, shortly after our second child, Michael, was born. We were so excited. Little did we know that I would be leaving Hasbro shortly thereafter for the West Coast.

I hired a local Sharon Realtor to find a buyer for the home. I gave him the exclusive listing and, more importantly, asked him to supervise the move since we would already be in Los Angeles. He assured us this was no problem and that he had done this many times previously.

Our final instructions to him were to be sure to move everything. He followed these instructions exactly. When the movers arrived in LA and began unpacking—we were renting in Encino on Coronet Drive—we discovered six large cans filled to the top with garbage, and this was well before recycling. He had truly packed *everything!*

Funny thing, the Realtor sold the house to Bernie Weiner of Halco Distributors, who was also in the toy business. I had even met him once or twice. Bernie was probably not happy with me once he realized that the house, which was set at the bottom of a steep driveway, was nearly impossible to reach in the winter. I heard later the driveway had to be electrified.

By the way, the driveway on Coronet Drive was not too much better. It had a small turnaround on a downward slope. These experiences resulted in us buying a house below the Encino reservoir as our next home purchase. It was on the very flat White Oak Avenue

DO YOU SMOKE POT?

We moved to LA from the Windsor Garden apartments in Norwood, Massachusetts, in late 1969. We didn't know a soul there.

Geri's close friend Amy said, "You must call my sister when you get there," which we immediately did.

The sister's first words after Geri introduced herself were, "Do you smoke pot?"

Geri said, "No, sister."

She immediately hung up, and that was our official welcome to La La Land.

FLYING PRIVATE
NOT AS GOOD AS IT SOUNDS

The Daisy Manufacturing Company formed in 1882 is the largest manufacturer of BB-caliber air guns. Their biggest seller, Red Ryder, was based on the Winchester rifle popularized in Westerns and a popular comic strip that ran from 1938-1963. Their business ended up being in trouble as a result of safety concerns with guns being in the hands of young boys.

I had a week of paid consultation with them and had to find a way to get to their remote headquarters in Rodgers, Arkansas. My flight started in Los Angeles, but that was the easy part. I remember nothing about the assignment. I do, however, remember the round-trip flights to and from Oklahoma City.

The plane taking me to Daisy was piloted by a very old WWII veteran, and he was piloting a biplane! It was the same two fixed wings stacked one above the other design that dates back to the Wright brothers.

It was a beautiful clear day for flying and I loved every glorious moment of the short flight. I was taken off guard by the biplane, but had no time to be nervous. A week later, upon my return, my legs were shaking but fortunately the flying weather was beautiful again.

I'M WEARING ED LEVY

I used to get the heebie-jeebies thinking about wearing the clothes of a deceased person that I knew well. All that changed when my dear friend Bobbie Levy, widow of Ed Levy, brought me bags full of Ed's clothing. They had all been cleaned and were neatly folded. Some had never even been worn.

Bobbie insisted I take what I wanted, and said that Ed would be happy knowing his clothes were being put to good use. Some of Ed's clothes fit my taste, and when friends admire the shirt and ask me the brand, I proudly say I'm wearing Ed Levy.

EMPLOYEES SPOIL
A TRADITIONAL GESTURE

My late brother-in-law, Steve Draizin, was one of the nicest, most caring, and smartest persons I've ever met. He was married to Geri's sister, Dolly, and was instrumental in getting us to move to The Valley of the Sun.

He was a principal in the oil distribution business, and RAD Oil, based in New Rochelle, was founded by his father Bob. As a gesture to the employees at the company, I decided to give out a turkey at Thanksgiving.

It seemed simple enough, but in a short period of time, handing out turkeys turned into a complex undertaking. There were just too many choices: fresh or frozen, what day to pick-up, and whether more than one turkey should be given if more than one family member worked for the company, etc.

Finally, RAD no choice but to discontinue the practice. Too much of a good thing had become a big pain in the ass.

Dwayne "The Rock" Johnson

ONLY PERSON IN AMERICA WHO DOESN'T KNOW WHO THE ROCK IS

I was traveling first class (a rarity) on a short flight from Houston to San Antonio to start a new consulting assignment. I began chatting with a good-looking hulk of a guy, talking mostly about football, my sweet spot.

Upon arrival at the airport, there were hundreds of girls screaming and holding signs that said, "The Rock, We Love You." I didn't think much about it; I was just anxious to get to my new client.

When I got there, I was introduced to my secretary who had a small office filled with pictures of The Rock. To my astonishment, I had unknowingly sat along side him on the plane. The Rock, AKA Dwayne Johnson, couldn't have been nicer. I told the secretary about the chance encounter and she almost fainted. When she'd recovered, she touched my sleeve, hoping the magic would rub off on her. What a way to meet your new secretary!

GOOD DEED
TURNS ME INTO A GIGLO

Arnold Green, a close college friend, was taking his fiancée to her high school prom. He asked me if I would be willing to take her best friend to the prom, since she did not have a date.

I knew this girl, but I had little interest, especially since it cost a lot of money to go to prom. There was the tuxedo rental, flowers, the after-prom party, etc.

Then the girls' father offered to pay me money to take his daughter to the prom, I thought it was a nice gesture. So, I agreed, thinking I was doing a good deed.

The $50 arrived with the understanding his daughter would never learn about the transaction. After the uneventful prom, I was verbally beaten up by my friends for being a Giglo.

Bob Hope on right with comedian pal Jerry Colanna

IMAGINE GETTING PAID
TO WRITE JOKES

I met an LA neighbor, Bob Sullivan, one day when we were both walking our dogs. Bob's full-time job was writing timely jokes for Bob Hope. He told me he had been doing so since World War II.

We became friends and I learned that writing jokes is a pressure-packed enterprise. Bob told me he was constantly competing with other jokesters. On the day before Hope went live, the FedEx truck showed up at his house every four hours for a joke pick up.

The last time I talked to Bob, he was writing jokes about Cleveland, where Hope would be making an appearance. My best off-the-cuff joke at the time was: "I'm so old remember when all t-shirts were white." The joke would never make the cut.

WIFE'S WILL POWER IS BEYOND THE PALE

I had gone to Hong Kong many times on business sourcing trips, but after the British left on July 1, 1997, many agents I did business with left the business and moved to Vancouver, Canada. Those who remained were forced to move to Mainland China (PRC) to be near their factories.

The train ride to the Chinese border near the modern metropolis of Shenzhen took about half an hour. Then you would then take a taxi to travel inland to the rural part of the country. When you did this, it was like you went back in time.

When Geri accompanied me on the journey, it was her first visit to Mainland China. We arrived at about 9 a.m., and I promptly went to work leaving Geri waiting in the reception area.

At about noon, Geri said she needed to take a pee and was escorted by a female assistant to the bathroom where she was expected to squat over a hole outside in the middle of the dirt. She said no way to this concept and waited to go back to the hotel.

When we got back to our room in the early evening, she promptly blew a kiss to the invention of indoor plumbing. She was extremely happy to go to the bathroom in the comfort of a five-star hotel room before going to dinner in one of what would become her favorite cities.

NEVER SEND A GENTILE TO BUY FRESH BAGELS

Fresh bagels at the NYC Toy Fair were mandatory for all showrooms in the toy building. The best place for bagels was H and H, and my apprentice Jason M. and I pulled up in a taxi and I sent him to purchase six dozen assorted bagels.

A short time later, out came Jason with bags full of freshly baked, warm bagels that had an irresistible smell. But all was not well. Jason mistakenly ordered six dozen salted bagels. It was an absolute disaster!

Customers wanted an assortment to choose from, like onion or poppy seed, with a smear of cream cheese. Then they would move on to the next showroom, promising to come back later. Some did, some didn't.

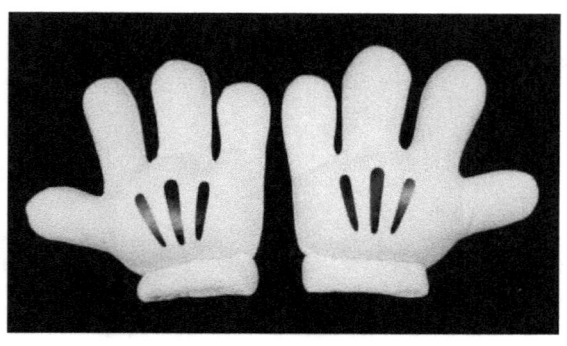

DID I REALLY WIN
THE BOSTON MARATHON?

The Boston Marathon, headed by Will Clooney of the BAA, is the it premier marathon in the world. It was an amateur event until the TCS New York Marathon was established in 1970 by the Road Runners Club. They provided prize money for the first time.

I had created a Boston Marathon game with Clooney's blessing. It was a traditional board game where the winner was the first to advance from the start in Hopkinton, passing Heartbreak Hill, to the finish line at the Prudential Center.

As part of the promotion, game designer Elliot Rudell had T-shirts printed with the words Boston Marathon Winner in large type, followed by the word game underneath in tiny print.

Bill Rodgers was a former world marathon record holder who won three straight at Bostons from 1978-1980. His trademark signature was running while wearing Mickey Mouse gloves. Rodgers had a store in the historic Faneuil Store Marketplace and agreed to promote the game. Part of the promotion included a fake run in which I beat Rodgers to the tape. It was publicized in the *Boston Herald*.

Jogging in the shirt during the actual marathon, I got booed by the pursuits, even though it was clear that at my very best I would finish light years after the elite wheelchair racers.

Groucho Marx lighting-up La Preferida,
his favorite Cuban cigar.

ENGLISH NOT SPOKEN
IN THE BOARD ROOM

Thanks to Rick Neitz, the president and CEO of Play-By-Play, I was preparing to attend my first board of directors meeting. I was employed as a full-time consultant, following Rick from DSI, where I was instrumental in getting the company sold.

I was an advocate for terminating a world-wide licensing agreement with Warner Brothers, giving the company exclusive licensing rights to their stable of characters. In my opinion, the deal was flawed and very one-sided. I called into question why the agreement was ever approved by PBP.

The founder of PBP was Arturo Torres, a Cuban refugee who made his fortune as a major franchisee for both Pizza Hut and Taco Bell. He was also the head of the board. Most of the board consisted of his friends, and only Cubano was spoken during meetings. This language is a distant cousin of Spanish, and is also referred to as Castilian Spanish, which is spoken exclusively in Spain.

Understandably, I was unprepared to make my case after getting a C grade in beginning high school Spanish. The only good thing about the meeting was the food and wine. The Lechon Asado was perfectly prepared and no Iron Chef was needed.

NYC PARKING SIGNS PURPOSELY CONFUSING

I was excited to find a free parking space in the early morning in front of IL Molino, one of the great Italian eateries on 86 West Third Street in lower Manhattan. I remember taking my time, studying the array of parking signs before leaving for a day of business, hustling, but mostly walking.

When I returned, I was surprised to find my car was gone (this was years before carjacking became fashionable). It had been towed to a huge parking lot set aside for this sole purpose. Apparently, I had not interpreted the signs correctly.

The tow lot was on the west side of town near the docks. When I arrived there, the line was long and filled with pissed-off New Yorkers.

It took me approximately two hours to get to the front of the line. When I was asked for my auto registration, I replied in a matter-of-fact manner that the registration was, of course, in the car. I asked the attendant where the car was, but he was clueless.

I said, "I assume that when I come back from retrieving my paperwork, I will jump back to the front of the line. Correct?" The attendant just laughed.

Four hours later, I left with my car and my wallet lighter by $75, about the same price as a meal at Il Molino.

LOST PET WORTHY OF
AN ALL-POINTS BULLETIN

O ne day, we were heading to the Jersey shore, which was one of our favorite destinations. We were about to reach Exit 98 on the Garden State Parkway (the last exit to the beach communities) and traffic was surprisingly light. Geri, Michael, his two kids, and his wife, Karen were in the car with me.

Karen got a call saying her dog had escaped from their residence in Westfield, New Jersey. It seemed the dog sitter, a relative, had looked the wrong way and the dog escaped. The sitter was feeling terrible and was at a loss as to what to do and where to go.

Karen, ever so smart, called the Westfield police department and they immediately went into action, issuing an all-points bulletin. Serious crime is hardly ever an issue in one of

Jersey's best places to live, so they had time to deal with the escapee.

We turned around and went home. Upon arrival, the police had the dog surrounded—problem solved. Shortly thereafter, we all relaxed and headed back to Point Pleasant, where my son has a summer place. This time, there was traffic, but we were in too good a mood to complain.

This reminds me of a business lunch I had at Balthazar with Lisa Sliwa, wife of Curtis, the head of the Guardian Angels. They're the guys with the red berets, who are volunteer crime fighters in support of New York's finest.

Lisa, who was active in the movement, opined about growing up in a small town in Indiana. She said a high crime and misdemeanor there was when two girls wore the same dress to the prom.

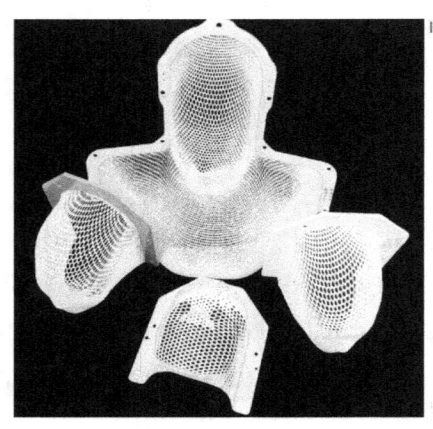

WHO WOULD WANT
A CANCER SOUVENIR?

Ihad a gel-like substance on the bottom of my right eye just above the lid, so I went for a series of eye exams at The Eye Center of Newark, New Jersey. This was just before I was diagnosed with orbital cancer after a biopsy was taken.

I was now patient diagnosed with cancer and my selected oncologist ran a cancer clinic at the Overlook Medical Center in Summit, New Jersey. Finding parking at this establishment was almost as stressful as the cancer therapy.

Targeted radiation therapy was the protocol I was given, and I was fitted for a custom thermoplastic mask that molded to my face and firmly held my head in place. I was then zapped, I believe 12 times, spread out over several months.

I was exhausted after the treatments and my eyesight hadn't improved. I felt I was in good hands, though. I remember how I felt after the last treatment: tired but relieved.

On the way out, after thanking the doctor, a nurse ran over to me and asked, "Would you like to take the mask home as a souvenir?"

I said, "Are you kidding?" I couldn't imagine anyone wanting a cancer souvenir.

The nurse said many take the mask home as a reminder of what they went through. I never wanted to see that mask again and walked out empty-handed. The thought of framing and displaying it in the living room was not my taste in terms of building an art collection.

My right eye's vision returned completely, but after several years, the scar tissue took over. I'm told this is a common occurrence. So, today I can't see anything out of the affected eye.

I go to periodic eye exams at Southwest Eye to make certain my left eye's vision stays intact. I'm happy to report that it's so far so good, thanks to the superb care of Ophtalmologist and world-class retina specialist Dr. Daniel Adelberg, assisted by scribe Nerida.

I still have a series of pictures taken of my right eye. It was a total waste of time, but it was also a protocol requirement. They said, "Doc says it's important that your eyes stay healthy."

My response was always the same: I would rather see than have a healthy right eye.

MAYO CLINIC

WORK WAS STRESSFUL IN THE MOST UNUSUAL OF PLACES

While working out at the gym at the upscale Legend Trail community in Scottsdale, I would on occasion meet a lovely lady who suffered from severe migraines. She was getting some relief from the medication Botox. She confessed the reason for the headaches: it was her job, which was much too stressful.

She told her employer this, but was offered no suggestions as to how to modify her workload. What's sad about this is, the lady worked at the Mayo Clinic—champion of alternative therapies. It's hard to make this stuff up, folks!

RESIDING IN A HOTEL ROOM
WITH A PET KANGAROO

Back in the 1980s, I did some consulting work for Brown Shoe's ROOS sneaker brand. ROOS had a distinctive zippered pocket on the side of the shoe that was perfect for holding change, keys, etc.

Their mascot was a kangaroo. So, I had a kangaroo stuffed toy designed, and the item was scheduled to be introduced at the upcoming Stationery Show at NYC's Javits Center. The company, for promotional purposes, had a pet kangaroo who lived with his trainer and traveled the country for store openings, trade shows, parades, and the like.

I arrived two days before the show, and spent a night in a hotel suite with the kangaroo and its trainer. I went to show management, with trainer and kangaroo in tow, and was advised that kangaroos are not on the approved list of animals allowed at the show. I found this strange, since as far as I knew, animals of all types were allowed. I definitely recalled seeing caged tigers and alligators. Who knew a kangaroo was more dangerous that those two animals!

EVERY COMMUNITY SHOULD
HAVE AN UNOFFICIAL MAYOR

E very resident of a community should be blessed with an individual like my good friend and neighbor KRT. KRT was born in Richmond, Virginia, but is an ex-New Yorker who loves the men's one-of-a-kind Paul Stuart clothing store just like I do.

KRT is suave, articulate, and an amateur meteorologist. He's well read (he even rents books from the library), a student of history, a lover of old Westerns, witty, and just a good guy.

KRT lives alone in a perfect apartment location where he can see all the comings and goings and provide advance notice of visitors, etc. to his friends. He has seen vandals before, during, and after their offenses; office personnel changes; he knew whether or not workers were showing-up or had been replaced, gave advance notice of work delays; and he saw problems with pavement resurfacing and water shutoffs, etc..

Just the other day, we had a power outage and KRT advised APS that our utility would have it fixed by 4 p.m. Today, he told us that the local branch of Bank America, which is within walking distance, had finally opened again after being closed since COVID-19 hit.

Author Howard G. Peretz

EPILOGUE

As you begin to age, many of us become preoccupied with creating a bucket list and then crossing off the items on that list one by one as they are achieved. The term Bucket List was created in 1999 by American and British screenwriter, Justin Zackman. Justin created his own Bucket List of "things to do before I kick the bucket."

I'm not a big believer in such a list. Life circumstances often get in the way, so an individual thinking about visiting the Taj Mahal mausoleum in Agra, India, may decide instead to get a successful hip replacement. A further problem is that if your list is too short, what do you do the following day? Or if your list is too long, will you get frustrated realizing your goals will never be realized?

Interestingly, most of these types of lists seem to have been prepared by a travel agent. My feeling is that internal or spiritual growth and living in the moment is a more rewarding path—it's the journey not the destination.

Throughout the book, I've made this point: people, not places, are where the action is (just like what's described in the 1964 Barbra Streisand hit "People," composed by Jule Styne, lyrics Bob Merrill).

I think you need to get up each day, bury your smart phone in your pocket, and venture forth. You should observe and hopefully interact with people, always being curious and learning about life.

"When you wake up each morning and stretch your arms and if you don't feel wood it's a good day" (courtesy of Dick Berlowe)

Howard Peretz

Howard Peretz

APPENDIX

LIFE LESSONS

The cliches are: youth is wasted on the young, and the best way to live is from the end to the beginning. Both are not plausible but what is possible is to reflect on your life learning what worked and what didn't.

The main focus of *Unusual Legacy* is looking at the world through a humorous lens. I, however, learned other life lessons as well that have been sprinkled throughout the text and their listing follows:

- Retirement is unhealthy—work is medicine without side effects.

- When working at home, dress the part.

- Practice the five P's: prior planning prevents piss poor performance.

- We are born with two ears and one mouth, indicating we should listen more and talk less.

- Less is more, except when you have something of substance to say.

- As the late playwriter and philosopher George Bernard Shaw said: "I want to be all used up when I die"

- Don't live to eat, eat to live.

- I have by necessity become a cheating vegan once I turned 80, but I still avoid dairy and sugar at all costs.

- To get the best service while dining out, review your tipping approach before the meal begins.

- When you cheat on your diet, make it a big cheat, say a hot fudge sundae, not a fun sized bag of peanut M & M's.

- Life is stressful and stress cannot be eliminated but you can do a multitude of things to reduce it. My go-to activity is Restorative Yoga

- Acupuncture can work if you give it time. The problem is that it is hard to find a good one as making a living difficult acupuncturist requiring herbs to be sold

- This quote from Henry Van Dyke Jr is right on the money when referring to COVID-19: "Some people are so afraid to die they forget to live."

- Buddhists believe between birth and death we are all alone so above all else be happy in your skin.

- The longest distance to travel is between the heart and mind.

- The best two words in English language in my case are: Cancer Free.

- This wisdom from the Japanese is true of winners in life: fall seven times get-up eight.

- Staying healthy is your responsibility not your doctors'.

- As you age, it's painful to break-in new doctors, so I try to choose health care providers in the 50s age bracket.

- Integrated medicine works only when the patient does the integrating: Western medicine is interested in symptoms, while Eastern medicine works toward prevention.

- Modern dentistry is still painful, the pain has moved from the mouth to the wallet

- Viktor Frankl, Holocaust survivor and author of *The Meaning of Life*, makes total sense. He says life's purpose is not to be happy but to be productive.

- Group therapy is effective because we all need a safe and compassionate place where last names are never revealed.

- I waited too long to take Viagra

- Reality: life is unfair.

- Reality: life is inconvenient.

- If luck is defined as preparation meeting opportunity, how then do the same people get lucky over and over again?

- To get the desired outcome, sometimes it pays to sit back and wait for events to occur.

- Purposely do something selfish daily, even if it's something a simple as going for a walk.

- I've tried learning how to relax, but have found that emptying my mind without falling asleep is most challenging.

- A friend of mine had the simplest way to describe aging: when you're young you want a BMW and when you're old you want a BM.

- It's almost impossible to find a capable doctor who is caring as well as competent. For example, I've had primary care doctors looking at blood work numbers who never looked at or touched me.

- I attribute the fact that my memory is still intact to religiously doing daily repetitive memory exercises

- Post-It notes eliminate the likelihood of the senior moment.

- Eliminate anxiety by taking a daily dose of cheap generic Xanax.

- As you get older, it makes total sense that days go by slower, while years go by faster.

- Spalding Gray: rejoice the moment it happens, not while looking back.

- I have this Chinese proverb framed on the wall behind my desk: Talk does not cook rice.

- There are two kinds of people: those who take risks entering the arena and those who watch (the majority). In my opinion, the number-one spectator sport in America is second guessing.

- Having a "bucket list: is a flawed concept. If you complete the list too soon you will have nothing to live for, and if the list is too long you live a life of frustration.

- Don't expect applause when doing something good.

- Surprises are wonderful in childhood, but can backfire in adulthood.

- Giving a gift card as opposed to purchasing a gift demonstrates you overvalue your time

- It's easier to give advice than receive it.

- Chasing green is a marathon race where you rarely reach the finish line.

- It's not abnormal being uncertain about the existence of God.

- Accept change and don't be afraid.

- Accept the fact you can make the correct decision while still getting the wrong outcome.

- When you realize you're not good at doing something, change or you will forever be stuck.

- Getting even or getting revenge sounds good at the time but is never worth the price.

- As Winston Churchill's political rival Aneurin Bevin said: "Politics is a blood sport."

- Corny traditions are better than a life without traditions.

- A principled vote for President would benefit all if there were a box on the ballot to allow you to vote for none of the above.

- Academic excellence finishes in second place to street smarts.

- The only problems you solve are those you create.

- A good idea precedes a great idea.

- Daily routine does not have to be boring. At the end of each writing day I play 1977's "Goodnight Irene" covered by Ry Cooder.

- Saving for a rainy day was invented by the insurance industry.

- Showing up is not close to being 90% of the outcome as advertised—it's what you do after arriving that separates the boys from the men.

- When you're angry, remember to first to count to ten before speaking.

- Treat a sunny day at the shore like a vacation.

- Meeting strangers is more interesting than travelling to far away places featured in tour guides.

- Individuals are not all equal, instead they are created uniquely.

- It takes smarts and courage to say I don't know.

- Don't scold yourself for being judgmental; it's a hill too steep.

- New ideas are fragile. It's much easier to say no than to take a chance on something untried.

- Bad news travels faster than good news.

- Listening to music is a beneficial mood changer that can immediately impact the creative process.

- I thought for years that movies were created for viewer enjoyment, never realizing the creators were more about advancing an agenda.

- Mother advised a white lie was acceptable when necessary; the problem is once you start telling lies you need to record them to keep them straight.

- I subscribe to the theory: perfection is the enemy of the good.

- Upon reflection, I'm too goal-oriented and should have learned to love the journey more.

- When you've been an empty suit it's difficult to move from telling subordinates what to do to asking them.

- I'm very sensitive and for years incorrectly went out of my way to hide it.

- Susan Boyle singing "I Dream a Dream" on Britain's *I Got Talent* gives courage to late bloomers.

- Seeing the play *Rashomon* as a teenager had a profound effect on me; it proves the non-existence of absolute or objective truth.

- I admit to being wardrobe superstitious when preparing for a medical appointment.

- Putting your pet dog down requires a period of mourning before deciding to rescue your next.

- While dogs do an admirable job of communicating non-verbally, I confess to dreaming out loud about how fabulous it would be if dogs could talk.

- Before proposing to Geri, I checked out her mother and she passed the test with flying colors.

- Internal beauty in your future spouse is more important than external beauty.

- I've been happily married for 61 years. When asked what my secret is, my honest response is that it must be chemistry.

- When competing in sports with younger athletes, especially hoops, gaining respect is more important than winning.

- When losing to an opponent, most rationalize and start looking for excuses. It would be refreshing to hear someone use my pet acronym LOFT—lack of talent—as the reason.

- I was a good club tennis player but when my skills declined I rejected the idea of playing old man's or social tennis.

- Late sports columnist Jimmy Cannon said, "Sports is the toy department of life." If that's true, why then allow politics to enter the arena?

- I advocate for making a game of in-person chess a required school subject.

- I'm a strong believer in compulsory military or equivalent training.

- I believe immigrants to America need to prefer assimilation to tribalism, just like the way this Jewish boy was taught.

- So-called combat pay is too high a price to pay for successfully climbing the corporate ladder.

- Grandparents should treasure grandchildren, not live through them.

- Saving stuff for your kids and their kids is a losing proposition. I think minimalism here to stay.

- Texting something of importance is an unacceptable way to communicate in my opinion. It seems designed for cowards.

- Assuming good health, living around young people and those with diverse back rounds is preferred to residing in a luxurious senior living ghetto.

- Getting there used to be half the fun. Today, flying sucks! My solution is to just fly the red eye and get it over with.

- A good friend is someone who rushes to your aid when you're down. So-called friends generally run away.

- My favorite Buddhist saying is: Turn arrows in to flowers.

- Never judge a book by its cover was stated originally by George Eliot (pen name for Mary Ann Evers).

- Settling for companionship rather than love in a second marriage is not the least bit settling.

- There's no such thing as a midlife crisis because your crisis can happen at anytime.

www.ingramcontent.com/pod-product-compliance
Lightning Source LLC
Chambersburg PA
CBHW070900120626
46546CB00001B/77